Scoundrels, Rogues and Heroes of the Old North State

SCOUNDRELS, ROGUES AND HEROES OF THE OLD NORTH STATE

Dr. H.G. Jones

Edited by

K. Randell Jones

Caitlin D. Jones

CHARLESTON   LONDON

History
PRESS

Published by The History Press
18 Percy Street
Charleston, SC 29403
866.223.5778
www.historypress.net

First published 2004

Manufactured in the United Kingdom

ISBN 1-59629-025-0

Library of Congress CIP data applied for.

Books by Dr. H.G. Jones include:
For History's Sake, 1966
The Records of a Nation, 1969
Local Government Records, 1980
North Carolina Illustrated, 1524-1984, 1984
North Carolina History: An Annotated Bibliography, 1995
Historical Consciousness in the Early Republic, 1995

Cover Illustrations
Front cover: Photograph of Tiny Broadwicke at Griffith Field in Los Angeles in 1913, courtesy of North Carolina Department of Archives and History.

Back cover, from left to right: Sam Brinkley, courtesy of UNC Photo Lab; Photograph of Annie Oakley, courtesy of Garst Museum; L.A. Scruggs, from his book *Women of Distinction, Remarkable Works and Inventive Character*, 1893.

Illustrations used inside the book:
'Fool Killer' from *Milton Chronicle*, March 10, 1859, courtesy of North Carolina Department of Archives and History; Line drawing of a doctor, source and date unknown; Line drawing entitled *Gathering*, source and date unknown; *Old Southern Schoolhouse*, from *Pictorial Field-Book of the Revolution* by Benson J. Lossing, New York, 1852.

Introduction

EVERYBODY LOVES A STORY. AND every person's life serves a purpose, even if only as a warning to others. Combine those two aphorisms and you get *Scoundrels, Rogues and Heroes of the Old North State*—entertaining stories about the heroes and the ne'er-do-wells who make Tar Heel history so colorful.

The tales in this book span four hundred years of North Carolina history, across the Golden Age of Pirates, the Colonial period, the American Revolution, the Antebellum years, the Civil War, Reconstruction, Prohibition, the early twentieth century and every era in between. They include stories of characters from the high seas, the coast, "down east," the mountains, the piedmont, the sandhills—every part of our state.

The stories in this special collection come from the *In Light of History* series by Dr. H.G. Jones. The series began recounting history and in the course of doing so became history itself. For seventeen years, from 1969 to 1986, Dr. Jones researched and wrote a weekly column at the request of the Associated Press. The enlightening and entertaining articles ran under the banner "In Light of History" in newspapers all across North Carolina. During nearly two decades, Tar Heels came to know themselves a little better through the insights to their collective past offered by these articles. They learned the who, the what and the why of social changes that have helped shape North Carolina across the centuries.

The sharing of these stories was a labor of love, for Dr. Jones was offered no compensation for his efforts. With an average of 6 hours research for each of 884 articles, he donated over 2½ years of 40-hour workweeks (5,300 hours) and wrote a half-million words that filled 17,680 column-inches of newspaper, enough to fill 134 newspaper pages without advertisements. During those seventeen years, he never missed a Wednesday deadline, whether he was in the hospital or hunting with the Eskimos. Yet he delighted always in sharing the stories in what he jokingly called a "bit of academic snobbery that said 'Hey, I bet you didn't know this!'" His greatest satisfaction, though, always came from providing a public service to North Carolinians interested in their history.

Great stories, wonderfully told by the state's premier historian: that's *Scoundrels, Rogues and Heroes of the Old North State*.

We are delighted to share these stories with you. If you remember reading them before, you know you will enjoy them again. If this is your first encounter with these tales, then we welcome you to North Carolina, with all its scoundrels, rogues and heroes.

KRJ and CDJ

Famous Imposter Bilked North Carolinian

JOHN CAMPBELL, EDENTON'S PROMINENT MERCHANT and member of the house of burgesses from Chowan County, welcomed the well-dressed stranger bearing the name Robert Middleton.

The visitor, according to Campbell, wore "drab lightish coloured coat, with Metal Buttons, [and] a pretty long black silk waistcoat." Physically, he was "a middle-siz'd smooth-fac'd Fellow, very smooth tongu'd, and is a pretty good Scholar."

Robert Middleton made a good impression upon the Edentonians, and when he produced a letter of credit from Colonel Andrew Meade (from up near the Dismal Swamp), Campbell handed him the money. Having partaken of Edenton's hospitality, the dashing young man left just before Christmas in 1744. It was only then that John Campbell learned that Robert Middleton was an imposter.

Ten months passed, and Campbell heard of another imposter making his way northward from the Neuse River settlements after landing in New Bern from Jamaica. This man called himself Captain Randall of the ship *Havanna*, but his description fitted that of "Robert Middleton."

The description also fitted Tom Bell, the news of whose frauds was spreading through the colonies. Consequently, from his Lazy Hill Plantation in Bertie County, Campbell inserted an advertisement in the *Virginia Gazette* offering a reward of "Five Pistoles, and all other Expences" to have the imposter committed to jail in Edenton or Williamsburg. Campbell added, "he [Bell] told some Gentleman when at Neuse River, fourteen days since, that he should make free with their Names, as it might suit has Conveniency in travelling Northerly: He has been in many Gaols to the Northward of Maryland." It is doubtful if Campbell ever recovered his money, for no record of an arrest in North Carolina has been found.

In 1745 John Campbell probably short-changed Tom Bell when he called him simply a "notorious Villain and Imposter." After all, historian Carl Bridenbaugh, in his book *Early Americans*, calls Bell "probably the best-known American both on this continent and in the British West Indies."

Born of a prominent Boston family in 1713, Thomas Wentworth Bell was expelled from Harvard University for theft at age twenty. Cut off from the usual careers of classically educated scholars, Bell adapted his education to a life of roguery. Making his way through the colonies, he committed deceptions that made him a celebrity.

Having been mistaken for an absent Presbyterian theologian in New Jersey, for example, Bell assumed the preacher's identity, accepted an invitation to deliver a sermon on Sunday morning, then on pretext of having forgotten his notes, went back to his host's home, ransacked it and rode off on a fine horse. The irate parishioners finally located the real minister and twice convicted him of robbery. The imposter, meanwhile, was carrying on his swindles in other colonies and in the West Indies.

To understand the success of such imposters, one must remember that in the first half of the eighteenth century there were no rapid means of communication and no photographic means of circulating likenesses of culprits. No newspaper was published in North Carolina until 1751.

Thus a community had little more than a visitor's word for his identity, for letters of introduction could be forged easily. Bell assumed a long list of identities. As John Campbell said, "he often changes his name, the better to impose."

Tom Bell's ultimate fraud was his announced plan to publish a book to be titled *The Travels and Adventures of the Famous Tom Bell*. By means of a large advertisement in the *Virginia Gazette*, he collected money for advance sales and then fled the colony. No book ever appeared.

Tom Bell spent much of the remainder of his life as an officer on ships in the Caribbean. He was about fifty-eight years old when his sloop captured a Spanish schooner near Cuba, plundered it and left it adrift with neither water nor provisions for the crew. For this crime the "famous infamous vagrant" Tom Bell "penitently" went to his death at the gallows in Jamaica in 1771. Few Harvard men ever attained equal fame.

The Hanging of Frankie Silver

ADRIVE BY THE OLD BURKE County Courthouse stirs recollections of history made on the square in Morganton. Built about 1835 by James Binnie from local cut stone, the handsome old structure has hosted the famous as well as the infamous.

Prior to the Civil War the August terms of the state Supreme Court were held there, in 1865 General George Stoneman's raiders prowled through, and its courtroom was the scene of many dramatic trials. The building possesses both historical and architectural importance, and it exudes great charm.

One of the most famous trials in Burke history took place in the county's first courthouse a few years before it was torn down to make way for the new one. Clifton K. Avery, former business manager of Broughton Hospital and avid local historian, traced the chilling story through old court records and published it in booklet form.

Around Christmas, 1831, Charles Silver (the name was often spelled Silvers) disappeared from his cabin on the Toe River. His neighbors became suspicious and, upon inspecting his house, found signs of blood around the fireplace and floor and pieces of charred bone in the ashes. Shortly afterward, according to legend, dogs dragged a portion of a torso from a hollow stump. The remainder of Charles Silver was never found.

The murdered man's wife, Frances, and her mother and brother, Barbara and Blackston Stuart, were accused of murder. The indictment charged that Frankie "with a certain axe of a value of six pence, which the said Francis [*sic*] Silver in both the hands of her, the said Francis, then and there had and held to, against, and upon the said Charles Silver, then and there feloniously, willfully, and with her malice aforethought did cast and throw," causing his death.

Barbara and Blackton Stuart were accused of being "present, aiding, helping, abetting, assisting, comforting and maintaining" Frankie in her grisly deed. The grand jury, however, found insufficient cause to try the mother and brother.

Frankie was found guilty at her trial in March 1832, and she was sentenced by Judge Donnell to be "hung by the neck until she is dead." The state Supreme Court upheld the verdict, but the appeal, plus the failure of Judge David L. Swain (who that year was elected governor) to show up for the September term of superior court, prolonged Frankie Silver's life for more than a year.

Then, ten days before her scheduled execution, there was a sensational development; Frankie escaped from jail, supposedly with the assistance of her father and uncle. A few days later, however, she was apprehended in Rutherford County, dressed as a man with her hair cropped.

Finally, on July 12, 1833, Frankie Silver mounted the scaffold on a hill at Morganton. Tradition has it that before the trap was sprung, she confessed and recited a fifteen stanza poem of which the most poignant portion goes: "There shall I meet that mournful face whose blood I spilled upon this place; with flaming eyes to me he'll say 'Why did you take my life away?'"

Frankie Silver's body was buried near the old Buckhorn Tavern nine miles west of Morganton. A modern tombstone announces her claim to fame: "Only woman ever hanged in Burke County."

Lewis Redmond—King of Outlaws

THE BOOK WENT THROUGH AT least three printings in English and one in German. It was called *The Entwined Lives of Miss Gabrielle Austin, Daughter of the Late Rev. Ellis C. Austin, and of Redmond, The Outlaw, Leader of the North Carolina 'Moonshiners.'* Its author was listed as Edward B. Crittenden, Methodist bishop of North Carolina.

Illustrated with steel etchings and first issued in 1880, the book told the story of Miss Austin, daughter of a Greensboro Methodist minister, who by trickery was convicted of theft in Virginia and was sentenced to the whipping post. Stripped to the waist, she was snatched from the public flogging by a mysterious Robin Hood who allowed her to return home.

Months later the young lady visited her cousin, a federal marshal at Asheville, North Carolina, and was astonished as she rode with him through the countryside to be accosted buy a band of moonshiners led by the man who earlier had rescued her.

She was even more astonished when the man shot the marshal dead and pinned on his body a card signed "Redmond" and carrying a pair of skulls and crossbones and the slogan "Thus do I punish my enemies." Taken as a captive to Redmond's cave, Gabrielle suffered various indignities and eventually was the object of a rescue effort by her old Virginia fiancé, Charlie Hashagen. Charlie was caught, but Gabrielle persuaded their captors not only to spare their lives but to let them go free. Good-hearted Redmond went back to making liquor and shooting revenuers.

Having ended one narrative, the author then gave Redmond's own account of his life of outlawry. He claimed to have been born in Mecklenburg County, to have attended Princeton University, and to have traveled in Europe. He turned to outlawry when his father, a member of the Ku Klux Klan, was murdered.

And a fearful outlaw he was. He claimed to have been "directly concerned" with killing fifty-four men (no women, thank you), including a judge, a United States commissioner and an even dozen federal marshals. In other words, anybody who tried to interfere with his practice of free enterprise in the liquor business.

At the end of the book Redmond saved a lovely "Miss Stevens" from a raging panther, took over the town of Asheville with two hundred armed man, held a big wedding and then "galloped off into the night."

Despite the claim of the author that "I emphatically endorse this narrative as true in every particular . . . the honest stamp of truth in every line," the book was a hoax. "Bishop Crittenden" never existed. Nor, apparently, did Gabrielle or Charlie. But "Major" Lewis Richard Redmond did indeed exist, though the real life character was almost as mysterious as the mythical Redmond.

In 1881, for instance, R.A. Cobb, who identified himself as a federal official of Morganton, published "the true life" of the outlaw. Describing Redmond as having a "wild and roving" disposition, Cobb reported that the man was a fairly middling moonshiner of Transylvania County whose fame spread after murdering Deputy Marshal Duckworth in 1876.

With his newfound image, Redmond became a celebrity among other moonshiners, but five years later he was captured, tried and sentenced to ten years in federal penitentiary in Albany, New York. Much of Cobb's story, however, is also uncorroborated.

Perhaps John Preston Arthur, in his *Western North Carolina*, published in 1914, came closest to the truth. He described Lewis Redmond as a common bootlegger who killed not a federal marshal but a deputized citizen by the name of Alfred F. Duckworth. Redmond served a time in prison, and upon release removed to South Carolina where he killed another man and was again jailed.

Like so much fiction, the book by "Bishop Crittenden" so distorted the story that the real Lewis Redmond will probably never be untangled from the myths that once were woven around his name. In this case, fiction is stranger than truth.

Was The Slave a Prince?

WHETHER HE WAS A GENUINE prince, we will never know. But that he was a literate Mohammedan with genial manners is attested to by tradition.

Prince or not, Omeroh (Moro, Omar Ibn Seid or whatever his real name) was certainly a curiosity at Owen Hill up the Cape Fear River from Elizabethtown. Unfortunately, until some scholar unearths more solid documentation on his life, we will have little to go on except hand-me-down information.

According to tradition, around 1810 John Owen (who many years later would become governor of North Carolina) obtained the release from the Cumberland County jail of a strange-looking, peculiar-talking, dark-skinned man who had been apprehended upon assumption that he was a runaway slave. And indeed he was, for shortly thereafter his South Carolina owner showed up to claim him. Owen, by then intrigued by the fellow who disdained association with the other slaves, bought him and began the slow process of identifying him by the expediency of teaching him English.

When the dark man was able to communicate, the mystery of the curious writing on his jail wall was clarified. He was a prince of the "Foulah" tribe on the Senegal River in Africa, he said, and he had been captured by an enemy tribe and sold into slavery to a Charleston planter. He was taken to a plantation in South Carolina where, unable to speak English, he was unable to explain his identity. Treated harshly as just another slave, he escaped, only to be seized by the sheriff of Cumberland County who, under state law, jailed him and advertised for his owner to come for him.

Confident that the man's claims were true, the Owens family treated him almost as a kinsman. He was assigned a servant, furnished a cottage of his own and allowed to go and come without restriction.

Having learned English, Omeroh adopted Christianity and was baptized into the Presbyterian Church. Upon his request, Owen obtained for him a bible in Arabic. This bible, so treasured by the prince, is now preserved at Davidson College. A number of his manuscripts—in Arabic—have been preserved in other repositories, along with a photograph made in his old age.

Not satisfied with having a bible in Arabic for his own use, "Uncle Moro," as the family came to call him, requested similar bibles be sent to his tribe in Africa. Governor Owen, through American slave traders, left word at African ports that "the words of Moses and Jesus" would be sent to any of the Foulahs who asked. Years later a missionary wrote that "the Lord carried out the desires of good Uncle Moro's heart and made him the means of sending the Bible to his tribe."

Following Governor Owen's death in 1841, Omeroh chose as his master the governor's brother, General James Owen, who showed him similar respect. When Omeroh died just before the Civil War, he was buried in the family cemetery at Owen Hill.

Governor Owen, incidentally, apparently could have been president of the United States. While serving as presiding officer of the national convention of the Whig Party in Harrisburg, Pennsylvania, in 1839, he was offered the vice-presidential nomination on the William Henry Harrison ticket. He declined. His substitute, John Tyler of Virginia, became president upon Harrison's death in 1841.

Francis Culpeper Married Three Governors

GOVERNORS MUST HAVE HAD A particular fascination with Frances Culpeper. After all, she married three of them. Or, maybe she simply liked to move around, for one of her husbands was governor of Virginia, another of Albemarle (later Carolina) and the third of Carolina (both North and South).

The gubernatorially attracted Frances Culpeper was born about 1634 at Jamestown, Virginia. In her eighteenth year she married Samuel Stephens of Bolthrope Plantation on the Warwick River.

Stephens rose to prominence in Virginia, and in 1662 he was appointed by Governor William Berkeley to the post of commander of the "southern plantations." Five years later he was commissioned governor of the County of Albemarle "and the Isles and Isletts within Tenn Leagues thereof." Thus for several years Frances probably lived with her husband in the wild and sparsely settled area on the north shore of the Albemarle Sound.

If so, she probably yearned for even the simple amenities of Jamestown, still only a half-century old and little more than an armed camp. There wasn't a public building or village in the Albemarle, and sixty acres of land was promised to English settlers who dared venture into the new territory.

Frances didn't have to stay there long, though, for in 1760 Governor Stephens died. Strangely, Sir William Berkeley, governor of Virginia and one of the lords proprietors of Carolina, qualified as administrator of the deceased governor's estate.

Berkeley took a fancy to both Stephen's estate and his widow. Within a few months Frances Culpeper Stephens became Lady Frances Berkeley. Among the property that Berkeley gained with his new wife was Roanoke Island.

Frances reigned as Virginia's first lady until, following Bacon's Rebellion, Berkeley was removed from office. He died in 1677 after returning to England.

Berkeley, incidentally had an interesting attitude toward education. He wrote, "I thank God there are no free schools nor printing . . . for learning brought disobedience and heresy and sects into the world, and printing has divulged them, and libels against the best governments. God keep us from both." Good thing he isn't living in the twentieth century.

Lady Berkeley, of course, inherited her husband's proprietary share of the vast Carolina territory. She sold it to four of the other proprietors in 1683 for £300.

Frances next married Philip Ludwell, a native of England but a prominent Virginia official. In 1689 Ludwell was appointed governor of that part of Carolina lying north and east of Cape Fear. A couple of years later he was commissioned governor of all Carolina and took up residence in Charleston, leaving a deputy in the Albemarle.

Charleston must have been better than the Chowan River country, and Frances probably liked it better. But Governor Ludwell made the mistake of ruling Carolina liberally, and the lord proprietors fired him. The unhappy Ludwell returned to Virginia, presumably with Frances, the champion governor-hunter, and there he managed a couple of plantations.

Frances was buried in the churchyard at Jamestown. Apparently she bore no children, but the daughter of Ludwell by a former marriage must have caught her fancy for governors, for she later married the governor of the Leeward Islands.

There is one more curious twist in this case of gubernatorial relations. The mother of Governor Stephens (Frances's first husband) later married John Harvey, who as president of the council, served as governor of Carolina in 1679 and who gave his name to Harvey's Neck in Perquimans County.

Amos Owens Made "Cherry Bounce" Famous

"CHERRY BOUNCE"—A CONCOCTION OF three parts whiskey, one part cherry juice and one part sugar—brought world fame to Rutherford County and its most illustrious citizen.

Back in 1902, Amos Owens was eighty-one years old and illiterate, but he had a story to tell. So he invited Melvin L. White to listen to him and his neighbors and to write his biography. A little fifty-five-page booklet, *A History of the Life of Amos Owens, the Noted Blockader of Cherry Mountain, N.C.* appeared the next year. Amos paid the entire cost of $80 for printing a thousand copies.

The booklet told of a man who believed deeply that a citizen had a right to make an honest living by refining the fruits of nature into a satisfying beverage. Owens paid dearly for his convictions. In fact, his courageous struggle against "red-legged grasshoppers"—his characterization of federal revenue agents—led to repeated prison terms and the destruction of at least nine of his stills.

Born in 1821 on Sandy Run in the Walls Church community of Rutherford County, Owens attended only a few days of school, then turned to odd jobs as "hewer of wood and drawer of water" until adulthood. A rough-and-tumble youth, he became adept at breaking horses and wrestling men. At the age of twenty-two, however, he decided to get married.

He rode over to Mr. Sweezy's farm and asked where Mary Ann was. When the father asked what he wanted with her, Amos said he had come to marry her. "Marry, the devil!" snapped Sweezy. Amos shot back, "No, I just want yer daughter."

In two more years, Amos and his bride had saved enough money to make a down payment on a hundred acres of land on Cherry Mountain in eastern Rutherford.

A few years later he added to his holdings until he—like George Vanderbilt— owned virtually a whole mountain.

The main source of his income was moonshine. Except for the cherry trees, the mountain grew little, and it was said that a crow flying over the area had to carry a canteen of water and haversack of rations.

At the age of forty, Owens joined the Confederate forces, first serving in the 16th North Carolina Regiment. He was discharged for "anasarca"—a sort of dropsy. He later joined the 56th Regiment and was captured at Dinwiddy and imprisoned at Point Lookout before being released with typhoid fever. When he recovered from that, he returned to his first love, distilling spirits. He was arrested on several occasions.

During Reconstruction, Owens became active in the Ku Klux Klan, and along with Randolph Shotwell and others, he was convicted of terrorism against a Republican. He was sentenced to six years in Sing Sing and levied a fine of $5,000.

Upon his parole, he returned to Cherry Mountain and resumed his old occupation. Arrested again for violating the federal revenue laws, Owens was sent back to Sing Sing, where he claimed that his old friends welcomed him with a torchlight parade. By the time he got back to Cherry Mountain he was a growing legend.

At his home on the mountain, he entertained friends from miles around. He started an annual cherry blossom celebration on the second Sunday in June—a festival that lasted for days and took on the appearance of a medieval tournament with athletic contests, games and military drills. Cherry Bounce was the favorite refreshment.

On his third trip to Sing Sing, Owens claimed that the superintendent welcomed him with open arms: "Amos, I knew you would not disappoint us."

Owens was about seventy years old when he was again hailed before Judge Robert Dick, who had sentenced him several times before. The judge made this plea to the aging bootlegger: "Three times you have worn the garb of a convict, and time and again have you been fined and imprisoned. You are said to be a man of noble impulses and many worthy traits of character. Your gray hairs should be a crown of glory instead of a badge of infamy . . . Amos, as man speaks to man, will you cease to violate the laws of your country and be an outcast of society?"

Touched by the judge's appeal, the old blockader responded, "Judge, I'll try." The courtroom erupted with applause, and the lawyers took up a collection and bought the defendant a fine beaver hat and a Prince Albert coat, both of which he wore proudly the remainder of his days.

Amos Owens may have mellowed in his old age, but he never yielded his belief that making moonshine was an honorable calling and ought not to be considered illegal.

He died September 18, 1906, and was buried at Walls Church in sight of his beloved mountain where "Cherry Bounce" was made famous.

Anne Bonney, Woman Pirate

NOT MUCH IS KNOWN ABOUT Anne Bonney (or Bonny), perhaps the most famous pirate of all times.

That is why Jim Wann and Bland Simpson could do with her as they pleased in *Hot Grog*, the delightful musical comedy first produced in Chapel Hill and then at New York's prestigious Phoenix Theater.

Wann, a Tennesseean, and Simpson, who grew up in Elizabeth City and Chapel Hill, North Carolina, portrayed Anne as the daughter of Charles Eden, the governor of North Carolina who certainly tolerated and possibly was in cahoots with pirates operating out of the tiny ports of North Carolina early in the eighteenth century.

Of course she was not the governor's daughter, but the story of her life is elusive. Even her maiden name is unknown. The traditional source has been Captain Charles Johnson's *A General History of the Robberies and Murders of the Most Notorious Pirates*, published in 1724, but modern scholars have questioned many of Johnson's observations.

Apparently Anne was born in County Cork, Ireland, about 1700 to a prominent but promiscuous lawyer and his household maid. Perhaps for the child to qualify for her paternal grandmother's estate the circumstance of her birth was kept a secret and she was regularly dressed as a boy.

When the truth finally came out, however, her father's law practice dried up, and her grandmother disowned the child. So he brought Anne to the South Carolina Lowcountry where he reestablished himself on a plantation.

It was in Charleston that Anne, by then a teenager, became fascinated by seagoing vessels and the men who sailed them. Ere long, she met and married one James Bonney, a former English navy man who had taken up piracy. Bonney sailed with his bride for the West Indies, and on the way she took a liking to shipboard life.

In the Caribbean, however, Anne was swept off her feet by a handsome young man by the name of Captain John Rackham, called "Calico Jack." She abandoned James and set sail with her new suitor. Because women were uncommon on pirate ships, Calico Jack dressed Anne as a young man. She enjoyed appearing to be just another young crew member. She also was thrilled with the life of a pirate.

Soon, however, she began to make advances toward another young sailor by the name of Mark Read. Calico Jack was quick to threaten to run his sword through Read, and at that point Mark decided that he had better share a secret with Anne; that he was not really Mark but Mary—Mary Read, another woman who for years had disguised herself as a male pirate. Anne's budding romance with Mark—or rather Mary—wilted immediately.

This revelation of the infiltration of women into piracy appears not to have caused undue commotion aboard, for the women proved to be entirely as courageous as the men.

In fact, when Jamaican forces finally attacked and boarded Rackham's ship, the two women were left on deck alone to fight the attackers. The men, including Calico Jack, retreated below deck. The captured pirates were taken to Jamaica and tried in November 1720. They were sentenced to be hanged, the men first.

Rackham was allowed to visit his unfaithful consort just prior to his hanging. Remembering his cowardice during their capture, Anne told him that if he had fought like a man, he would not have to be hanged like a dog.

When it came time to fix the date of the women's execution, both told the court, "My Lord, we plead our bellies."

Mary and Anne were pregnant, and under English common law an unborn child could not be killed. Their executions were postponed. Anne was eventually released from prison and allowed to return to Charleston where she faded from public view. Her name, however, still conjures up visions of a bloodthirsty female pirate who was more than a match for any of the men who dared to test her.

"Mr. Read" Was a Woman

L IKE HER SHIPMATE ANNE BONNEY, Mary Read had an unusual childhood, spent part of her life disguised as a male pirate and eventually was sentenced to be hanged.

Mary's mother was the wife of an English sailor who had been at sea more than a year before the girl was born. Her illegitimate birth, therefore, was hidden from the sailor's relatives. However, when a legitimate son, just a year older than Mary, died, the mother decided to dress Mary as a boy and pass her off as the legal male heir.

Thus it was that Mary Read became disguised as Mark Read who, at the age of thirteen, was hired out as a servant. Not liking this work and "growing bold and strong, and having also a roving mind," Mark went aboard a ship, ended up in Flanders and joined an infantry regiment. Soon Mark quit the infantry and joined the cavalry, earning praise from the officers.

But Mark was really a Mary, and the soldier fell in love with another member of the regiment. When Mary revealed her sex, the fellow was elated over the prospect of having a mistress in his tent. But Mary had another idea. She withheld her favors until the soldier agreed to marry her. The marriage of the two troopers "made a great noise," and their comrades raised funds to enable the couple to leave the service.

They opened a tavern near Breda and for a time prospered. The husband died, however, and Mary resumed her male disguise and boarded a Dutch man-of-war for America. The ship was captured by English pirates who, recognizing "Mr. Read" as English but not as female, took her to the West Indies.

There the English were organizing privateers to attack Spanish shipping, so Mark Read joined up. When the ship got to sea, however, some members of the crew, led by Captain John ("Calico Jack") Rackham, deposed the officers and ran up the flag of piracy. It was aboard this vessel that Anne Bonney and Mark Read discovered that they were both women, a secret shared for a while only with Rackham.

But again love won out. Read became attracted to a shipmate, a "forced man"— that is, one who had been captured and forced to serve as a member of the crew. To the great surprise and delight of the young man, Mark confessed to being Mary, and they agreed to be married when they returned to port.

In the meantime, though, the male lover became involved in a quarrel with another shipmate and was challenged to a duel. Mary realized that her suitor was the weaker of the two, yet she could not allow him to be branded a coward.

To save her fiancé from almost sure death, the disguised Mary intervened in the quarrel and issued her own challenge to the adversary. Not suspecting Read's motive, the antagonist accepted the challenge. They chose sword and pistol. Read killed the opponent on the spot. This courageous act confirmed the crew's respect for the toughness of "Mr." Read, who fought shipmates and enemies alike.

Not long afterward, a ship representing the governor of Jamaica overtook Rackham's vessel and demanded its surrender. Bonney, Read and one other member of the crew remained on deck to fight the boarding party, but they were no match for the well-armed attackers.

Taken to Jamaica, the women revealed their sex and were given a separate trial for piracy. Both were sentenced to be hanged, but both, being pregnant, appealed to English common law, which prevented the taking of the life of an unborn baby.

Consequently, their sentences were stayed. Mary died in prison, perhaps in connection with the birth of her child.

Naomi Wise
Memorialized in Song

A T PROVIDENCE FRIENDS MEETING A simple tombstone reads "Naomi Wise" with the dates 1789-1808. Not far away is Naomi Wise Spring. Farther down Deep River at Randleman are Naomi Street, Naomi Falls and Naomi Mills. And the name of Naomi Wise has been immortalized in song. In recent times Doc Watson of Boone popularized it again.

Judged from the breadth of its diffusion, said the late folklorist Frank C. Brown, *Poor Naomi* (sometimes titled *Omi Wise*) is North Carolina's principal single contribution to American folk song.

The original song went through many changes as it was handed down from generation to generation in rural areas as far away as Missouri. In fact, it was localized in many instances, thus erasing its association with Randolph County.

After several generations, some North Carolinians came to doubt the legend of Naomi Wise. Perhaps, thought some, it was the figment of the fertile imagination of a novelist. After all, it seemed to have been published first in the *Greensboro Patriot* in 1874 under the fictitious byline of Charlie Vernon.

But the doubters should have searched the records, for they could have traced the original story to Braxton Craven, the respected principal of Union Institute, who published it first in 1851 in an obscure literary magazine, *Evergreen*.

And, if they had searched long enough, they would have verified the tragedy in the court records of Randolph and Guilford Counties. For the body of Naomi was indeed found in Deep River in 1808, and Jonathan Lewis did stand trial for her murder.

Admittedly, Craven went far beyond the facts particularly when he created long conversations between the lovers. But he had been born only fourteen years after the murder, and he grew up in the company of neighbors who vividly remembered and talked about the horrible story. The Methodist teacher was unworried about libel, for the tradition of Jonathan's guilt had to him become fact. Furthermore, Lewis had confessed the crime on his deathbed, and a dead man couldn't recant.

Naomi Wise was a poor orphan girl who was taken in and raised by the William Adams family in the community of New Salem in northern Randolph. Across the Guilford County border on Polecat Creek lived a family named Lewis, the menfolk of whom were noted for their good looks, strength and ruthlessness.

Young Jonathan Lewis took a job clerking for Benjamin Elliott in Asheboro. The road from his home in Guilford to Asheboro passed near the Adams cabin, and Jonathan became attracted to the pretty young lass in the household. In fact, he fell in love with Naomi, and they became engaged.

Meanwhile—according to Craven, at the urging of his mother—Jonathan began paying attention to Hetti, the sister of the wealthy Benjamin Elliott. It was a convenient arrangement: Jonathan had a girlfriend at Asheboro during the week and another at New Salem on the weekend.

As his courtship with Hetti progressed, a nasty rumor spread from New Salem that Naomi was pregnant. The accusation of having seduced Naomi threatened Johnson's plans to marry Hetti, so publicly he denied involvement. But privately to Naomi, Jonathan Lewis professed his love and his plans to marry her.

According to Craven, "Naomi urged the fulfillment of his promise, that he would marry her forthwith, seconded by the power of tears and prayers. When these means seemed unavailing, she threatened him with the law. Lewis, alarmed at this, charged her . . . to remain silent; he told her that their marriage was sure, but that very peculiar circumstances required all to be kept silent."

Finally, Lewis set the date. Rejecting Naomi's request that they be married at her foster father's house, Jonathan instructed her to meet him in secret and he would take her to a magistrate where they would be wed quickly and without fanfare. Then they could return to the Adams house as man and wife.

On the appointed evening, Naomi slipped out of the house on the pretext of going for a pail of water. Jonathan met her at the spring, and from a stump that for generations was to remain a monument to her memory, the nineteen-year-old girl mounted the horse with him.

Her previous doubts of Jonathan's love and faithfulness must have vanished as they rode off toward their nuptials.

Naomi Wise Rode Off to Death, Not Marriage

NAOMI WISE MUST HAVE BEEN the happiest young woman in Randolph County when she climbed upon Jonathan Lewis's horse that evening in 1808. At least the ugly rumors of Jonathan's unfaithfulness would be laid to rest, and her child would be born in wedlock.

It was later in the evening, after dark, that a Mrs. Davis, who lived several miles down Deep River near the present town of Randleman, heard a series of loud screams from the direction of the river ford. They were unmistakably the cries of a woman in distress.

Mrs. Davis and her sons, carrying torches, rushed to the ford. Hearing a horse galloping off the opposite side of the river but seeing nothing, they returned to the house, puzzled by the incident.

Meanwhile, William Adams and his wife worried all night about the disappearance of their foster daughter. The next morning, finding the empty pail and hoof prints at the spring, they called upon their neighbors who joined in tracking the horse.

Along the way they met Mrs. Davis who told of the occurrences the night before. Almost without hesitation the disappearance of Naomi and the screams in the dark were connected, and foul play was suspected.

A brief search in the shallow river yielded the awful truth; Naomi Wise had been drowned. Her dress had been tied above her head, telltale proof of murder. All suspicions centered on Jonathan Lewis, and a search was begun. Late that night, after tracing his route all day, the searchers found him at the home of Stephen Huzza, sitting before the fireplace and holding Martha Huzza in his lap.

While Jonathan Lewis was awaiting trial, he escaped from the "shackley frame jail" in Asheboro and disappeared. Though unavenged, the murder of Naomi Wise was not forgotten in Randolph County, and the song "Poor Naomi" (or "Omi Wise") spread far beyond the county's borders.

Nearly seven years later word was received in Randolph that Jonathan Lewis had settled in Kentucky. Determined to bring the suspect to justice, Sheriff Isaac Lane deputized Colonel Joshua Craven and George Swearengain, and the three set out for Kentucky. There they hired two hunters to lure and capture the strong escapee.

Lewis was returned to Asheboro and again jailed. This time great care was taken to prevent his escape. But Lewis's lawyers exploited the obvious emotionalism of the community and succeeded in having the trial moved to Guilford County.

At Greensboro the state made a good but circumstantial case. There had been no eyewitnesses, and after seven years memories were sometimes confused and conflicting. The jury acquitted Jonathan Lewis, who rushed back to his Kentucky home.

He never seemed the same after the trial, and his last years were spent in sadness. On his death bed Jonathan Lewis confessed his crime to his father. On the pretext of taking her to a magistrate, he had lured Naomi away to drown her without trace so that he could marry Hetti Elliott.

In the middle of Deep River, he grabbed her by the throat, and it was at that point that Mrs. Davis heard the blood-curdling screams. The couple fell from the horse into the river, and with brute strength Jonathan held the struggling girl in the water until all resistance ended. Seeing the flares in the distance, he spurred his horse up the opposite bank and hurried off.

Had Naomi Wise lived a normal life, she might never have been heard of beyond Randolph County. Her name, however, is now memorialized around the world by the song, which begins:

"Come all ye good people, I'd have you draw near,
A sorrowful story you quickly shall hear;
A story I'll tell you about N'omi Wise,
How she was deluded by Lewis's lies."

Otto Wood,
Famous Prison Escape Artist

OTTO WOOD WAS JUST THIRTY-one, but his name was already well known among law enforcement officers of the country. After all, he had been in and out of their hands since he was only seven years old. An escape artist, some folks called him. That is why he was in solitary confinement at Central Prison in Raleigh in 1926. Superintendent George Ross Pou was determined that he wouldn't break out again.

But Wood seemed to have reformed, and he spent his time writing. Finally, the prisoner asked permission to have his manuscript published as a pamphlet. Pou read it, doubted its sincerity, but agreed to its publication. A lot of other people, though, were touched by the twenty-seven-page booklet titled *Life History of Otto Wood, Inmate, State Prison*. In it the author described how, following the death of his father, he "seemed to be different from the other boys in the family, ruthless, so they say."

His life of crime was launched when, at the age of seven, he ran away from his Wilkes County home and took up with an uncle at Vulcan, West Virginia. Not only did the lad learn a lot hanging around the uncle's saloon, he also witnessed several of the feudal battles between the Hatfields and the McCoys.

The first serious trouble came on a visit to his mother in Wilkes. Jailed for stealing a bicycle, he and a fellow inmate planned to steal guns from a Wilkesboro hardware store as soon as they were released. Caught a second time, Otto was sentenced to an Iredell County chain gang before he was old enough to shave. By the age of thirteen, the youngster had been involved in a list of minor violations of the law. At that point, however, he tried to settle down to a job in a West Virginia coal mine. At seventeen he became a locomotive fireman and lost his left hand in an accident.

He married one woman but was sent to jail for breaching the promise to another. He escaped and fled to Texas, Arizona and Mexico where he acted as a "tough easterner," wore two guns, gambled much, drank heavily (because "it seemed to ease my restless mind") and got into many fights.

In succeeding years Wood compiled a monotonous record of arrests and escapes from Mexico northward and eastward. Moonshining, fighting and stealing. But he had not yet been accused of murder. That void in his record was filled in 1923 when he was convicted of killing A.W. Kaplan of Greensboro in a pawnshop holdup. Wood was sentenced to thirty years in Central Prison. He averaged an escape per year, until Superintendent Pou threw him into solitary.

Wood's little book was a sort of preachy document intended, he wrote, as a means of "helping some fallen mortal to a higher life." It brought such public sympathy that the prison directors ordered him released from solitary confinement. This kindness was repaid by another escape on November 22, 1926. Wood promptly wrote Governor McLean that he would surrender if he received a promise of treatment commensurate with his stature as a high-class prisoner. The governor just as promptly doubled the reward for his recapture.

It was not long in coming. At Terre Haute, Indiana, Wood was wounded and arrested in an attempted burglary. North Carolina had to rush to get in front of Ohio, Virginia and perhaps other states, all demanding his extradition.

Back in Raleigh, Otto Wood again was placed in a solitary cell along death row. By 1929, however, reformers began decrying his confinement. He was interviewed by social workers that called him "a neat, healthy, rather well-built man" who, presumably, didn't like being in prison.

The famous criminal even attracted the attention of Governor Max Gardner, who visited him and listened to Wood's latest claim of remorse and reform. The governor announced an "experiment in humanity"; he ordered that Wood be given the full privileges of an "A" grade prisoner. In return for being put in charge of the prison canteen and zoo, Wood promised, "I'll never run away as long as you are governor." That was May 20, 1930.

On July 10, Otto Wood simply disappeared from Central Prison. No one knows how. For nearly six months he was a hunted man. Then, in Salisbury on New Year's Eve, 1930, Police Chief R.L. Rankin and his assistant, J.J. Kessler, were driving along the streets. They spotted what they believed to be a familiar pedestrian.

When the officers approached him the man drew a pistol, announced that he was Otto Wood, forced himself into the car, and ordered the chief to drive out of town. Instead, both officers drew their own guns. In the ensuing gunfire, North Carolina's "most notorious criminal" died. He had failed in his eleventh—and most important effort to escape.

North Carolina Governor Married Fifteen-Year-Old Girl

IN COLONIAL TIMES IT WAS not unusual for a fifteen-year-old girl to get married. Nor was it unusual for a seventy-three-year-old man to take a second wife. But when they married each other, that was news. Particularly when the man was the royal governor of North Carolina.

The child bride was Justina Davis, who married Governor Arthur Dobbs in 1762. Then, after his death, she married Abner Nash, who became the second governor of the independent state during the Revolution. Circumstances surrounding the courtship of Governor Dobbs and the pretty teenager are unclear.

In a letter purportedly written in 1762 by a North Carolinian to a friend in Maryland, it was stated that, "Our Old Silenus of the Envigorated age of Seventy Eight who still Damns this Province with his Baneful Influence grew stupidly Enamored with Miss Davis a Lovely Lady of sprightly fifteen of a good family and some Fortune." The writer went on to claim that Justina's planned marriage to an eighteen-year-old lover was broken up by the governor who forced her to wed him instead.

The tone of the letter and the addition of five years to the governor's actual age, however, leads to the suspicion that the message was more of a vicious political attack upon Dobbs than a factual account of his courtship and marriage.

Furthermore, Justina appears to have been a devoted wife who took good care of the aging governor when he suffered a stroke within a year after their marriage. "My dear Jessy," as Dobbs called her, in 1764 sent Dobb's children in Britain a barrel of Carolina rice and a box of spermaceti candles.

Though the governor never fully recovered from his stroke, he was able to attend to his duties and do some traveling. In 1764, however, he asked to be relieved, and the crown sent to North Carolina a young lieutenant governor named William Tryon.

Now that the governor was being replaced, the assembly, with which he had quarreled frequently, adopted conciliatory statements expressing appreciation for ten years of "unwearied endeavors to serve his [the king's] interest and the Province."

Dobbs wrote his son, Conway, that he would leave for London in March 1765, and that Jessy would go with him. As spring approached, Jessy excitedly began packing the governor's possessions in their home, Russellborough, at Brunswick. Then, just a couple of weeks before they were to sail, Governor Dobbs suffered another stroke. Two days later the old man died in Jessy's arms.

To her stepson, she wrote, "Alas I have lost my ever dear Mr. Dobbs which makes me almost inconsolable . . . I have lost one of the best and tenderest of husbands and you a kind and most affectionate father." Justina buried the governor in St. Philips Church at Brunswick, only a short walk from Russellborough.

As an attractive and eligible eighteen-year-old widow, Justina could have had her pick of many new suitors. She chose Abner Nash, a popular twenty-six-year-old attorney and legislator from Halifax.

When the sons of the deceased governor refused to pay Justina the £2,000 willed to her, Nash, her new husband, went to court. The case involved the right of Americans to lay claim to property owned by British citizens who had never lived in the colonies, and the outcome had a bearing on a lengthy controversy between Governor Josiah Martin and the colonial legislature.

Justina bore Nash three children before she died in 1773, still only twenty-six years old. At this young age she had married one governor, and her surviving husband, Abner Nash, would become governor seven years later.

Justina was buried in Halifax. Nash remarried and lived until 1786 when he died in New York while attending the Continental Congress. He was buried there in St. Paul's churchyard, but his body was later interred again on his plantation, "Pembroke," near New Bern.

Thus Justina lies buried alone, more than one hundred miles from the graves of her two husbands, both governors of North Carolina.

Malinda Blalock, North Carolina's Only Female Civil War Soldier

DURING THE COURSE OF THE Civil War, North Carolina provided approximately one hundred forty thousand soldiers for Confederate service. Of that number, 139,999 were in many ways unremarkable, at least in comparison with one, whose name was Malinda.

Sarah Malinda Blalock Pritchard, alias Sam, North Carolina's only known female Civil War soldier, was the wife of William McKeeson (Keith) Blalock and was living "under the Grandfather" in Watauga or Caldwell Counties at the outbreak of the war.

Keith, although a Union sympathizer, enlisted on Company F 26th Regiment North Carolina Troops, March 20, 1862, to avoid conscription and in hopes of escaping to the Union lines. "Sam" Blalock, actually twenty but described as "a good looking boy, aged 16," enlisted on the same date.

For the next two weeks Private Sam Blalock "did all the duties of a soldier" and was, we are told, "very adept at learning the manual and drill." The new private tented and messed with Keith, who was presumed to be a brother, and watched the other men when they went swimming near Kinston. It was observed, however, that Sam never went in.

Keith, meanwhile, speedily grew tired of soldiering and having endured the military life for a few weeks, "went into the bushes and covered himself with poison oak," or, according to another account, poison sumac. The army surgeons, however, although puzzled as to the nature of his disease (one story said leprosy was diagnosed), agreed that he was unfit for service, and he was granted a discharge.

Private Sam Blalock then presented himself to an incredulous company officer and, in a manner which is lost to posterity, "disclosed the fact" that he was a woman. Private Malinda Blalock was then, according to various company and regimental records, "immediately discharged" and was "sent home rejoicing."

As far as is known, Malinda's disguise was never penetrated, nor her sex suspected during her brief career as a Confederate soldier. Had she remained in the army, Malinda ultimately might have been found out, but given the apparent obtuseness of her officers, this appears doubtful.

As one of the latter gentlemen observed acutely, perhaps with his colleagues' guffaws still ringing in his ears, she was after all, "dressed in men's clothing." How was he to know Malinda was a woman?

The story of Malinda—or Sam—is just one of the many interesting accounts turned up by Weymouth T. (Hank) Jordan Jr., editor of the *Civil War Roster* for the Division of Archives and History. The seventh volume, which covers the 22nd through the 26th North Carolina regiments, carries the story of Private Samuel Blalock.

Rains Brothers of New Bern

Two brothers, natives of New Bern, became the Confederacy's leading experts on explosives during the Civil War, but because both spent most of their adulthoods outside the state, they are seldom remembered as Tar Heels.

Gabriel James Rains and George Washington Rains were sons of a New Bern cabinetmaker, Gabriel Manigault Rains, and his wife, the former Hester (or Esther) Ambrose. Both were educated in the New Bern Academy, then were selected as cadets in the United States Military Academy. In the Civil War, Gabriel and George served the Confederacy as high-ranking officers.

Gabriel Rains graduated from West Point in 1827 and was given an army commission. He was wounded and decorated for gallantry in the Seminole War, and he participated in the Mexican War. When the Southern states seceded from the Union in 1861, Lieutenant Colonel Gabriel Rains of the Union army became a brigadier general in the Confederate army.

For years he had been experimenting with explosives, and when he was placed in charge of a brigade at Yorktown the following winter, he mined the waters. When in the spring his troops were forced to retreat, he planted shells and percussion fuses along the roadway, causing casualties among the pursuing Union soldiers.

This first use of land mines in warfare brought outraged cries from Federal officials and the Northern press. Many Southern officers, gentlemen even in war, were also indignant over the use of so ruthless an invention, which caused such indiscriminate deaths. Confederate James Longstreet forbade their use against the enemy.

A great debate ensued among Confederate leaders. Finally, Secretary of War

George Randolph decided that it was all right to use the land mines "in a parapet to repel assault, or in a road to check pursuit," but he rejected their use "merely to destroy life."

The controversy brought General Rains to the attention of President Jefferson Davis who was enormously impressed by a small, black object that looked like a lump of coal. The device, concocted by Rains, was designed to be slipped into the coal supply of enemy vessels.

Its effectiveness was demonstrated when one of the camouflaged bombs was shoveled into the boiler of a captured blockade runner, the *Greyhound*, which was carrying Union General Benjamin Butler and Admiral David Porter. Both officers escaped the explosion and subsequent sinking, and thereafter a close watch was placed around all Union coal supplies.

President Davis then appointed Rains to the position of superintendent of the Confederate Torpedo Bureau. Soon he built torpedo (mine) factories at Richmond, Wilmington, Charleston, Savannah and Mobile, and supplied mines—some of them weighing nearly a ton—to protect the James River from Federal ships.

More Union ships were said to have been lost during the war from mines than from all other causes. Rains himself claimed that his mines sank at least fifty-eight enemy vessels. In his native state, Rains' mines sank seven of twelve Federal ships on the Roanoke River. His land mines helped Fort Fisher hold out until early in 1865, thus keeping open the South's most important lifeline until the last four months of the war.

His land mines were crudely but ingeniously constructed. One type involved a small buried powder keg protected from the rain by a conical tin roof over which was laid a small plank, itself half-buried. One step on the plank set off the explosion. Another type was triggered when a foot soldier tripped over a hidden cord. Around Richmond alone, Rains' men planted nearly 1,500 mines. After the fall of the city, Southerners who knew how to locate the mines had to lead their captors through the mined fields.

After the defeat of the South, General Rains lived in Atlanta. Later he was clerk in the quartermaster department, stationed at Charleston. He married Mary Jane McClellan, a granddaughter of Governor John Sevier of Tennessee, and they had six children. The general died in Aiken, South Carolina, on August 6, 1881.

In subsequent wars dozens of nations improved upon this weapon of death first pioneered by the New Bern native whose brother was simultaneously serving the Confederacy as a supplier of gunpowder.

James H. Jones,
The President's Valet

"The many years which have come and gone since we have parted have in nowise diminished my regard for you and interest in your welfare." So wrote the former president to an old confidant whom he had not seen since the two were captured together by enemy troops twenty-four years earlier. Now, within a year of his death, Jefferson Davis was mailing a photograph "in order that you might see me as I now am."

James H. Jones entered the lives of the Confederate president's family in the summer of 1862 when Varina Howell Davis was evacuated from Richmond on the approach of Federal troops. The first lady took up residence with her sick child in the Yarborough House in Raleigh. Later she moved to one of the rock houses on the campus of St. Mary's School.

Prominent citizens recommended to her a young "free man of color" who, though a bricklayer and plasterer by trade, often spent his winters as a valet. The bond between them was warm, and when President Davis beckoned her back to Richmond in late summer, Varina engaged James Jones as her personal servant and coachman. He quickly became an accepted member of the household.

As the Union troops again threatened the Confederate capital in March 1865, the president sent his family southward for a second time. James Jones loaded upon one of the cars of the special train the two horses given to Varina by Richmond citizens. He and a maid were to care for Mrs. Davis and her children in their exile. Varina and her small party took up residence in Charlotte, North Carolina, expecting to return to Richmond as soon as the Yankees were driven away again.

In early April, however, President Davis himself fled Richmond, stopping at

Danville, Virginia, long enough to issue his last proclamation, then proceeding to Charlotte, where he rejoined his family and held his last cabinet meeting.

With the collapse of the Confederacy, Davis sought to escape. With his family and a small retinue, he crossed South Carolina and camped in the woods near Irwinville, Georgia. There in the early hours of May 10, James Jones, dutifully awake all night and with Davis's horse saddled, detected the approach of Federal troops. He hastily aroused the camp and sought to help Davis in his getaway. But it was too late. The party was captured, and both the president and the coachman were taken to Fortress Monroe, Virginia.

Upon Jones's release, he became the object of pursuit by Union forces. Major General H.W. Halleck reported on June 3, that Jones had "gone south via Raleigh, where his mother resides, for the purpose of obtaining two bags of money concealed near the place where Davis was captured." Apparently Jones neither recovered the rumored treasure nor revealed its whereabouts for he returned to Raleigh and settled into the life of a revered leader of the black community.

James H. Jones was born about 1831 to James and Nancy Jones, a free couple of color in either Wake or Warren County. Following the war, he attended two freedman's conventions, joined the new Republican Party, served as grand deputy of the Union League and as deputy sheriff of Wake County and was chief doorkeeper for the convention of 1868.

In 1873 he was elected to the first of several terms as alderman for the city of Raleigh. He was an organizer and first foreman of the Victor Hose Company and in 1876 helped form the first Negro military company in the state. Jones worked for at least two railroads and in 1887 was the first overseer of the Raleigh street railway. A few years later he took a job in the stationery office of the United State Senate, where General William Ruffin Cox of North Carolina was senate secretary.

Upon hearing of President Davis's death in December 1889, James Jones wired the mayor of New Orleans, "As the old body servant of the late Jefferson Davis, my great desire was to be the driver of the remains of my old master to their last resting place. Returning [to Raleigh from Washington] too late to join the state delegation from this city, I am deprived of the opportunity of showing my lasting appreciation of my best friend."

Varina Davis remembered that disappointment in 1893 when her husband's body was exhumed and sent to Richmond for reburial, stopping along the way for memorial services. At Raleigh she instructed that James Jones—whom she had first met there thirty-one years earlier—be permitted to drive the elaborate funeral car from the train station to the state capitol.

James Jones was finally a happy man. Later Varina sent him her husband's walking stick, and before he died at the home of a physician son in Washington, D.C., on April 8, 1921, he donated it to the Museum of History in Raleigh.

One of the South's Last Duels

AHANDSOME SHAFT RISES NEARLY TWENTY feet in Wilmington's Oakdale Cemetery, and its inscription reads, in part: "Sacred to the memory of Dr. William Crawford Willkings, who departed this life May 3, 1856, aged 30 years and 19 days . . . Dr. Willkings naturally attracted to himself the esteem and regard of a large circle of admiring friends who anticipated for him a bright career of future usefulness."

That career, the inscription adds, was "suddenly closed, and the hopes founded upon it buried with him in his untimely grave." The words "suddenly closed" veiled the story of how Willkings came to his death. The young doctor was, in fact, one of the last victims of dueling in the South. Like so many duels, this one was caused by the passion of politics.

In the 1850s, politics was a deadly serious subject to many Americans. Slavery was splitting the North and South, and the Whig Party was disintegrating. To oppose the Democratic Party, many former Whigs helped form the American or "Know Nothing" Party. The newly organized anti-slavery Republican Party, was of course, anathema to the South.

In Wilmington, the "Know Nothings" showed unexpected strength in 1856, and all races—even for offices like commissioner of navigation—were taken seriously. On the night of April 30, the courtroom was filled for a meeting of the local Democratic Party, headed by Dr. John D. Bellemy. Eli W. Hall, a prominent lawyer, was one of the spirited speakers.

Another was Dr. Willkings, who derided the "anti-Democrats" who sought to promote the idea of "pure Americanism." He appears to have said some particularly harsh things about Joseph H. Flanner, a "Know Nothing" candidate. The "Know Nothings" were not idle, and Flanner appears to have made cutting remarks about the "Sand Hill Tackies," meaning the Democrats. There was much excitement—and some incitement—on election day.

Of the five commissioners of navigation seats, each party won two. The fifth seat went down to the wire before Flanner won by a single vote over Miles Costin, the margin, according to the local paper, being a confused Democrat who cast the wrong ballot.

In the heat of the election, Flanner published a card branding as false some of the charges made by Dr. Willkings the previous night. Such cards or handbills were then a common way of making and answering charges. Apparently Flanner's was rather sharp, for Willkings challenged him to a duel.

Flanner expressed his willingness for a "fair and honorable settlement" without resorting to firearms, but Willkings rejected his offer. So the men and their "seconds" rushed to Marion, South Carolina, so that they would not run afoul of North Carolina's anti-dueling law. There, far from their homes, William Willkings and Joseph Flanner took up their pistols, marched ten paces and turned to face each other.

Flanner claimed later that his first shot was fired in the air, hoping to end the affair without damage, but when Willking's bullet grazed his arm, there was no compromise. Flanner's next bullet cut through his opponent's hat, and his third pierced the lung of Willkings, who in a few minutes died at the age of thirty.

It is not clear who "won" in the final analysis, for the local paper reported that the remains of the young doctor were followed to the cemetery by "the largest and most deeply affected concourse of people that had ever been seen in Wilmington."

Flanner showed genuine remorse and during the Civil War was the Confederate government's ambassador at large in Europe. He moved to New Bern and died there in 1885.

Woman Buried Seated in Chair

T HE SIMPLE CROSS READS ONLY "Nance." More is said on a larger family monument nearby in Wilmington's historic Oakdale Cemetery. That family monument reads: "Nancy Adams Martin, died May 25, 1857, aged twenty-four years and twenty-one days. John Salter Martin was lost at sea, September 1857, aged thirty-four years. They were the eldest son and third daughter of Silas H. and Margaret Martin."

Even that, however, fails to tell the tragic story of Nancy Martin, who was buried seated in a chair, and John, whose body was never recovered from the sea. We are indebted to the late Louis T. Moore, who saved much Wilmington history, for the details. Silas Hosmer Martin was an antebellum businessman, shipper and captain in North Carolina's port city. Though a strong family man, he nevertheless enjoyed being at sea for long periods of time. In 1857 he planned an around-the-world voyage on his clipper ship, carrying freight from port to port. In addition to a crew including his son John, Silas Martin agreed to take along his daughter, affectionately called "Nance."

After three months of the voyage, however, Nance fell ill. With no medical help at hand, the young woman died on May 25, 1857. The grief stricken father and brother could not bring themselves to bury Nancy at sea; yet, they were on the high ocean, far from any port. Like most ships in those days, Martin's clipper carried large casks of whiskey, rum and other alcoholic liquids. To preserve Nancy's body, the Martins decided to store her body in one of the casks. It occurred to them, however, that a body would be tossed around in the liquid as the ship reacted to the angry waves of the ocean, and this prospect was disquieting to the father and brother. It was then that they devised a plan to hold Nancy's body rigid, no matter how much the ship was buffeted by the seas.

They took a strong oak chair from one of the cabins and lashed the body to the chair in a seated position. The chair was then placed in an empty cask and nailed carefully so as to make it immovable within the barrel. After the container was filled with alcohol, it was tightly sealed and a memorial service was conducted. Now that the corpse could be preserved indefinitely, the elder Martin decided that the ship should continue its voyage, fulfilling its contract to carry freight to its destination. No need to turn back to Wilmington until the mission was complete.

This decision was to haunt Silas Martin, for in September, four months after Nancy's death, the ship ran into a violent storm, during which John Salter Martin was swept overboard. His body was never recovered. The father could go no farther; instead, he changed his course and began the slow, sad trip back to Wilmington. Docking the vessel at the foot of Princess Street, Silas Martin stepped ashore and made his wobbly way to his home, carrying the first word of the double tragedy that had struck.

After considering how best to handle the precious cask that had survived the rough seas, the family chose to bury the body of Nancy Adams Martin just as it had rested for many months. A large hole was dug in Oakdale Cemetery, and the cask—still containing Nancy's body, seated and lashed to a chair, the entire contents preserved in alcohol—was lowered into it.

Sam Brinkley Was the Authority on Pogonotrophy

THE NAME OF SAM G. Brinkley is not found in biographical dictionaries. Yet few North Carolinians ever appeared before larger audiences in the United States and Canada. Even fewer had their pictures printed on widely sold postcards.

Sam Brinkley has been dead for more than half a century, but old timers in Mitchell County remember the good-natured man and his unusual physical characteristic. And if the youngsters doubt the stories about Sam Brinkley, they can go into the cemetery of the Presbyterian Church at Buladean and see for themselves, for there Sam's tombstone exhibits a recessed photograph of the community's most famous son.

Sam Brinkley was perhaps the world's greatest authority on pogonotrophy. That's right, pogonotrophy, the science of beard growing. Sam didn't start out to be an authority. As a young man he simply became disgusted with the speed with which his beard grew. Twice a day he had to shave the stubble from his face. So, in his early twenties he got mad and quit shaving, his wife's protest to the contrary.

His beard grew and grew—down to his chest, down to his navel and down to his waist. His students, in particular, were amused by their teacher's lengthy beard. So were travelers who came through Mitchell County. But sometimes the beard got in his way, and Sam decided he ought to be compensated for the inconvenience. So he had a pouch sewn on to his shirt, and he tucked his beard into the pouch. It stayed there until somebody offered him a dime to show it off. For a crowd the charge was a quarter.

By the time Sam was about forty, his beard reached the floor and was still growing. That was when the Barnum and Bailey Circus persuaded him to go on tour. For two decades Sam spent his summers traveling with the circus in forty-two states and several Canadian provinces, displaying his beard to thousands of people.

The beard finally stopped growing when it reached three inches beyond floor level. Sam had finally conquered the whiskers that he had decided to give free reign decades before. A picture postcard, showing the tip of the beard touching the floor, was sold wherever the circus went. For a time Sam exhibited himself at museums in northern cities.

Sam Brinkley was born a twin on September 21, 1850, near Burnsville in Yancey County, but two years later his family moved to Snow Hill near Ledger in Mitchell County. He farmed and taught school at Big Rock Creek near Buladean, a village formerly known as Magnetic City but renamed for Beulah Dean, daughter of the postmaster. There he married Vista Street. They had three sons—Marshall, Gus and Hoy.

While on an exhibition in Canada, Sam was visited by King Edward VII of England, who presented him with an autographed picture of himself and his own luxurious beard. Sam undoubtedly autographed one of his post cards for the monarch. Brinkley was a popular, outgoing man who enjoyed singing and practicing ventriloquism. He died at age seventy-nine on December 13, 1929.

Was The "Human Fly" a Tar Heel?

THE *CALGARY HERALD* OF SEPTEMBER 23, 1921, described a phenomenon: "In the whole history of Calgary no such crowd has ever gathered within its boundaries as that which assembled in the neighborhood of the Herald building Thursday evening to witness the most exceptional display of nerve and skill ever seen in this part of Canada."

The story described the scaling of the building's wall by the "Human Fly," dressed in white trousers, tennis shoes and a gray cap, as fifteen thousand people looked on breathlessly. The daredevil, according to the reporter, "flirted with death by purposely slipping at intervals and catching himself with his hands on a sloping windowsill or a precarious looking piece of stone decoration." He paused on the seventh-story windowsill and stood on his head, dangling his feet out over the crowd. At the top of the building he repeated the stunt, then climbed to the top of the flagpole two hundred feet above the ground and sat on the large brass ball reading the five o'clock edition of the *Calgary Herald*.

A few nights later the "Human Fly" thrilled another crowd of fifteen thousand people by scaling the wall of the ten-story Palliser Hotel blindfolded. Near the top of the structure he mounted a bicycle and rode the length of the building along the jutting ledge hardly a yard wide. Next he climbed the swaying flagpole, spread himself across the brass knob, and kicked out his legs and arms.

The buildings in Calgary were not much of a challenge for the "Human Fly" who claimed to have been the only man who ever climbed the exterior of the tallest building in the world at the time, the Woolworth Building in New York City. It was said that he scaled the entire seventy-five stories in an hour and a quarter.

The sure-gripped climber scaled the Wrigley skyscraper in Chicago in zero-degree weather before an estimated fifty thousand people. After that he demonstrated his skills in other major cities.

What does the "Human Fly" have to do with North Carolina? Just this: He claimed to have been Bill Strother, a Tar Heel. Frankly, we think there is something fishy about his story. There are two reasons. First, Strother claimed to have grown up on two different places in North Carolina—at Fayetteville, and at Steinville, near "Kingston." We have been unable to identify a place called Steinville, and any self-respecting Tar Heel wouldn't put a "g" in Kinston.

Second, much of what was published about Strother (sometimes spelled Strothers) was written by Chief Buffalo Child Long Lance who at the time was a popular columnist and folk hero in Canada. Recently, in his fascinating book titled *Long Lance*, Professor Donald B. Smith of the University of Calgary has unmasked the "chief" as Sylvester Chahuska Long, a native of Winston-Salem, North Carolina. Somehow, we believe that Bill Strother may have built a myth around his past too.

But Strother's story is too good to be ignored. Chief Buffalo Child quoted Strother as saying that he climbed his first building in Fayetteville and then practiced on structures in Raleigh. His name got in the papers, and he returned home expecting a hero's welcome. Instead, he was snubbed as a disgrace to the community. Strother apparently swore to get even with his neighbors.

In the North his exploits won him widespread publicity and, presumably, wealth. To publicize the Victory Bond campaign at the outbreak of World War I, the government gave him a special railroad car and a brass band and sent him across the country to attract crowds of American patriots. When he found that his itinerary would carry him through Fayetteville, Strother saw to it that citizens of the town knew in advance that their famous native son would be arriving at a certain hour for a hero's welcome. Thousands gathered at the station to make amends for their previous rudeness.

But as the train approached Fayetteville, the "Human Fly" whispered to the conductor who delivered the secret message to the engineer. Strother then instructed the brass band to take a position on the observation platform. Strother himself went back to his compartment and pulled down the shades. At fifty miles an hour the train sped past the waiting throng as the band played "Hail, Hail, the Gang's All Here." The "Human Fly" had repaid the snub, and he never returned to Fayetteville. Perhaps we will never know whether Bill Strother was really a North Carolinian.

Cyclone Mack Was Famed Evangelist

"GOD CALLED ME WHEN I was a little boy, and he don't make mistakes." That is the way Baxter Franklin McLendon, a fiery evangelist of the 1920s remembered by many North Carolinians as "Cyclone Mack," explained his conversion.

But the late Dr. Edward W. Phifer of Morganton, in an article in the *North Carolina Historical Review* tells the story a little differently. Born in impoverished circumstances on April 14, 1878, near Little Rock, South Carolina, the youngster followed his father as he "shifted about" tenant farming around Bennettsville, South Carolina and Rockingham. He was exposed early in life to what has been described as the "orgiastic" religion of the era, and at the age of fourteen he went with his father to hear the traveling evangelist, Beverly Carradine. McLendon later recalled that Carradine "laid his hand on me, a poor illiterate child of a tenant farmer," and from that time he felt "called to preach."

Apparently, however, it took a while for the call to take hold. As he grew older, McLendon entered into a "seamy sort of existence, for the most part dominated by gambling, drinking and bootlegging." At the age of twenty-one he climaxed an argument with the operator of a small Bennettsville grocery store by shooting him down in his place of business and leaving him for dead. Fortunately for him, the grocer recovered, and McLendon was required to stand trial.

Later, as a young man in Bennettsville, he kept books in the store of Colonel S.C. McCall, who had recognized him as a "natural born salesman" and sent him to business college in Augusta, Georgia. In addition to keeping the books for McCall, McLendon served as an agent for a photographic firm. He also became involved in the local liquor traffic.

After several brushes with the law, McLendon crossed over the state line into Richmond County, North Carolina, "just ahead of the warrants." After teaching in a "writing school" and peddling a book referred to as a "business guide" in Richmond County, he traveled to Florida where he worked as a saloon keeper, a palmist and a professional gambler before returning to Wadesboro, North Carolina, and opening a barber shop.

According to Phifer, the turning point in McLendon's life came in 1907 when he "wandered half drunk into a tent revival meeting where, after seventeen nights at the alter he was converted by Bud Robinson, the cowboy preacher from Pasadena, California." Asserting that "nothing except for Christian religion brings men closer together than booze," McLendon stopped carrying a gun, threw away his cards and dice, vowed to desist from fighting game chickens and set out to spread the gospel. Many who knew him, however, say that he never gave up the use of liquor as an aid in "bringing men together."

The people of Bennettsville, where he moved after living in Wadesboro for two months, raised money to send McLendon to the seminary at Asbury College in Kentucky and Moody Institute in Illinois, but he turned out to be a flop at preaching by book-learned techniques. Finally deciding to abandon conventional methods and "just be myself," he set out on an individualistic career speaking at backwoods churches, mill villages and at the South Carolina penitentiary whenever invited.

After twelve years of preaching, McLendon was still largely ostracized by his fellow South Carolina Methodists. In search of new acceptance he "eased over" into North Carolina where, as his biographer puts it, "the flower came into full bloom."

Phifer's article deals primarily with Cyclone Mack's 1920 revival in Morganton, but it also relates incidents from other "meetings" such as the time McLendon interrupted his crusade in Clinton to accept the challenge of a carnival wrestler who, it is said, usually demonstrated his powers on apes rather than evangelists. McLendon reportedly returned to the pulpit and continued his sermon $15 richer for the victory.

The revival in Morganton is said to have attracted large crowds to the four-thousand-seat tent almost every night for a month—including at one service the membership of the Ku Klux Klan dressed in their full regalia. Over one thousand conversions were claimed, and the collection totaled almost $9,000 and three coon dogs. It was described literally as a howling success.

In addition to Phifer's article, more information about McLendon can be found in his biography written in 1928 by Walter Barr, a McLendon staff worker who lived with the McLendons in Bennettsville for a considerable time; and in "The Story of My Life," one of McLendon's famous sermons written in 1923. He died in 1935 and is buried in Bennettsville.

"Indian Chief"
Was North Carolinian

CHIEF BUFFALO CHILD LONG LANCE became a legend. He outran the famed Jim Thorpe, turned down a rare presidential appointment to West Point, became a hero in World War I, won fame as a Canadian journalist, received good reviews for his lead in a motion picture and was called by Irvin S. Cobb the "Beau Brummell of Broadway."

When he shot himself to death in Los Angeles in 1932, Long Lance probably hoped to carry his secret to his grave. But Assistant Professor Donald B. Smith of the University of Calgary uncovered the truth: Long Lance was not the full-blooded Blackfoot Indian of Montana that he claimed to be. In fact, he was Sylvester Chahuska Long, born in 1891 in Winston, North Carolina.

Both of Sylvester's parents, Joseph S. and Sallie Carson Long, were part Indian, but in the nineteenth-century South their mixed blood forced them to follow the segregated patterns of blacks. The father worked as a janitor at a white school. Fortunately for his future, Sylvester inherited physical characteristics associated with Indians, and when he was twelve years old, he left home with a traveling Wild West show. From that time forward, he passed as an Indian.

Five years later, Sylvester returned to Winston long enough to persuade his father to sign his application to Carlisle Indian School as a Cherokee. When he arrived at the Pennsylvania school, however, the Cherokee refused to consider him one of their brothers. Sylvester nevertheless was a superior student and athlete, graduating in 1912 at the head of his class. Among his lifelong friends was Jim Thorpe, who lost to Long in three successive three-mile races.

Long next attended Dickinson College and then St. John's Military Academy, and at both places he earned top marks. His record was good enough to attract the attention of President Woodrow Wilson who offered him one of his six presidential appointments to West Point in 1915. Long declined the appointment and instead went to Canada and enlisted in the army as a sergeant under the name of B.C. Long Lance. He thus took on a new identity, and within weeks he was on the battlefield of France where he was promoted to lieutenant, won commendation for bravery and was twice wounded.

For recuperation and discharge, Long Lance chose Calgary, Alberta, where he soon became a reporter for the *Calgary Herald*. He covered all types of stories, but his articles on the Indian tribes became his specialty. Like no white man, he was welcomed by the Indians who furnished him colorful descriptions of their old ways. He was photographed in full Indian regalia, and he wove an intricate tale of his own origin among the Blackfoot Indians of Montana.

Later he joined two Vancouver papers, and his articles were carried in large American magazines such as *Cosmopolitan*. In 1927 he published his shocking story, "The Secret of the Sioux," in which he reported that General George Custer committed suicide during the height of battle. The publicity surrounding the Custer article led to a fictionalized book on the Blackfoot Indians. By the time it was published in1928, the book was advertised as the autobiography of Long Lance and the myth surrounding his life grew larger.

Next came the movies, and he played the lead in *The Silent Enemy*, released in 1930. Though the picture was not commercially successful, Long Lance received excellent reviews for his part. In New York, Long Lance was described as the "social lion of the season" by one columnist. But his fame was his undoing, for his past soon caught up with him.

His family in Winston-Salem had silently watched his success with both pride and resentment. When his father became ill and destitute in 1930, Walter Long traced his brother down in New York and gave him the news. The trip was not in vain, for the son soon began sending money to help his father. He also helped out Jim Thorpe, who was in financial straits. But Long Lance's new world had been invaded, and he seemed no longer able to find satisfaction in life. In 1932 he went to Los Angeles and shot himself to death in the home of a friend.

It was discovered that Chief Buffalo Long Lance—really Sylvester Chahuska Long—had given away practically everything he had earned. There wasn't even enough to pay for the return of his body to his hometown, and he was buried in the British Empire veteran's section of Inglewood Cemetery in Los Angeles.

Loud Hymn Singer
Taken to Court

WILLIAM LINKHAW WAS A STRICT and loyal member of the Methodist Church in Lumberton, a man of exemplary deportment. He was a happy man, and he liked to sing his praises to the Lord. Singing in church was one of his greatest pleasures.

But that was what got him into trouble. His singing was definitely not one of the greater pleasures of the remainder of the congregation. The problem was that William Linkhaw sang loudly, but he did not sing well. He sang so loudly and so poorly, in fact, that he was arrested and convicted of disturbing his fellow worshippers.

Witnesses in the case, including the Reverend Neill Ray, testified that Linkaw's voice rang above everybody else and was heard after all the other singers had ceased. Things got so bad that the preacher began to read the hymns rather than allow them to be sung. Subtle suggestions from his fellow churchmen were not heeded. It was his duty to sing loud to praise the Lord, he said. Maybe the trouble was that the others weren't singing enthusiastically enough. Maybe they ought to follow his lead.

Linkhaw's singing made part of the congregation laugh and the other part mad. Some of them got so mad that they took him to court for disturbing the congregation. The judge for the case in Lumberton in 1872 was Daniel I. Russell, later to become governor of North Carolina. Recognizing the uniqueness of the case before him, Russell asked for a demonstration of Linkhaw's hymn singing. Linkhaw was happy to oblige, and cut loose. The judge, jury, attorneys and spectators were convulsed with laughter. No longer did they have doubt; William

Linkhaw, regardless of his piety and loyalty, did indeed disturb the peace. Found guilty, Linkhaw was fined one penny. Outraged, he appealed to the North Carolina Supreme Court, which heard the case in the fall term of 1873.

The dignified Supreme Court soon recognized that Linkhaw's singing caused a disturbance of considerable proportion. On the other hand, even the prosecution conceded that it was not the man's intention or purpose to bring misery to the congregation. In fact, it was admitted that he was conscientiously taking part in the religious services. The Supreme Court, with rare insight, ruled, "It would seem that the defendant (Linkhaw) is a proper subject for the discipline of his church, but not for the discipline of the courts."

His conviction was overturned. One wonders, however, if in their deliberations the justices might not have counted their blessings for not being members of the congregation of the Methodist church in Lumberton.

Annie Oakley
Thrilled Pinehurst Residents

Sitting Bull called her "Little Sure Shot." Will Rogers called her "the best known woman in the world." Her neighbors at Pinehurst simply called her "Annie."

In fact, Annie Oakley wasn't her real name, but by that name she thrilled two generations of Americans and charmed North Carolinians among whom she lived for seven years. Still another generation flocked to movies and Broadway plays based upon her career and featuring such stars as Barbara Stanwick, Ethel Merman and Betty Hutton.

In the popular mind, Annie Oakley was associated with the Wild West. But she was really an Ohioan. She was born Phoebe Ann Oakley Moses on August 13, 1860, in a log cabin in Darke County, Ohio. By age ten, Ann Moses demonstrated unusual talents with firearms, and it is said that she shot and sold enough wild game to pay off her widowed mother's farm mortgage. Her career—and her shortened name, "Annie Oakley"—began when at age fifteen she met an Irish immigrant showman, Frank E. Butler. Annie not only joined Butler's shooting act, but also became his wife the next year.

In 1885 Frank and Annie joined the national touring show of Colonel William F. "Buffalo Bill" Cody, and for sixteen years Annie was said to have missed only four performances. It was with Buffalo Bill's Wild West show that Annie Oakley almost lost her life in North Carolina. On October 29, 1901, as three trains carrying the show sped from Charlotte to Danville, Virginia, a southbound freight pulled out and into the second train near Lexington. In the head-on crash, Annie was seriously injured and Buffalo Bill lost many horses. His losses were put at $60,000.

But Annie recovered, though she and Frank resigned from the Wild West Show and began their own shooting exhibitions. Her name was virtually a household word in the English-speaking world, and she held gold medals from many competitions.

In 1915 Annie and Frank signed a contract with the Carolina Hotel in Pinehurst. She gave exhibitions and shooting lessons, and Frank managed the skeet range. A local editor wrote that the name Annie Oakley was a "synonym for cool and accurate fire—rifle, pistol, shotgun, standing, running, upside-down, at any target from a moon beam to a meteorite."

Suddenly, shooting became a fashionable sport for lady visitors to the resort town, and Annie Oakley was the chief drawing card. Dressed in tweeds, laced boots and feathered hat, she was the belle of Pinehurst. At a hotel ball, Annie won the costume prize by dressing as "Sitting Bull, Jr." Several thousand persons received shooting lessons from Annie Oakley, including eight hundred in 1921 alone.

During World War I, Annie toured army camps and was immensely popular among the soldiers. She and Frank also raised funds for the Red Cross, but often the star of the show was Dave, their bird dog. Dave sat calmly while Annie shot potatoes from atop his head; he also was trained to sniff out money which, when found, was turned over to the Red Cross.

After leaving Pinehurst in 1922, Annie was badly hurt in an automobile accident in Florida. Though it was feared that she would never shoot again, within two years she was at May View Manor at Blowing Rock where she broke ninety-eight out of one hundred clay pigeons.

From 1922 to 1926, Annie and Frank spent most of their time in Leesburg, Florida. Her health deteriorated, however, and they moved back to Ohio where, on November 3, Annie died. Frank Butler was so distraught that he too died twenty-three days later. They were both buried at Brock, Ohio, not far from the birthplace of Phoebe Ann Oakley Moses.

Ruben C. Bland,
Champion Papa

RUBEN C. BLAND WAS INDIGNANT. Some fellow from Georgia, the father of twenty-eight children, had been introduced all around Washington as the "champion father" of the country.

"Humph," Ruben Bland is reported to have scoffed, "he had only twenty-eight. If the president smiled when he saw him he'll go into hysterics at the sight of me." That was all that Carl Goerch, then editor of the *Washington Progress* (North Carolina), needed to hear. He contacted Congressman Lindsey C. Warren, arrangements were made, and on January 6, 1927, Ruben Bland took the spotlight in the nation's capital.

Here is how the congressional record quoted Congressman Warren on the floor of the House of Representatives:

Today, when the national defense of the country is being debated, it is fitting that we stop again and pay tribute to a man who has and is contributing more to the man-power of the nation than any other citizen.

Incensed and indignant that one would be so bold as to attempt to usurp his well-earned laurels Ruben C. Bland, of Robersonville, Martin County, N.C., my most famous constituent, has come to Washington and sits yonder in the Speaker's gallery.

He is the father of 34 children, and this wonderful accomplishment has been the subject of song and poetry for many years. (Applause.) He stands in a class alone. He is the champion father of America. He is a walking advertisement of the great section of the country from which he hails.

Warren recalled that former representative John H. Small, after the birth of Bland's twentieth child, had offered a suit of clothes for each subsequent one, and that "fourteen times was Mr. Small called upon." The congressman then quoted a telegram received from a Kansas City woman: "Ruben, Ruben, I've been thinking, you are quite a nifty man: to your health I now am drinking—you have done what few men can." The members, invited to see "what a real father looks like," cheered loudly when Ruben Bland stood and bowed.

Shortly afterward, the record-making father was escorted by Warren, Goerch and Jonathan Daniels to the White House.

When told that the North Carolinian was a father of thirty-four children, President Coolidge heartily shook his hand and gave this characteristically reserved comment: "Mr. Bland, you should be thankful for the many blessings that the good Lord has bestowed upon you." Responded the champion daddy, "Thank you, boss."

Down in Elizabeth City, crusty old editor W.O. Saunders tried to pooh-pooh the publicity coup of his rival editor, maligning the hero as "this procreant bull of the Martin County hinterlands . . . [who] has laid around home for half a century and made a stud record that would provoke only a mirthful hee-haw of contempt from a two-year old jackass."

Saunders claimed that once Bland took his family to the fair in Williamston and was trying to line them up to see a champion bull when the manager rushed out and said, "Wait a minute, Mr. Bland, we want to bring the bull out to see you." "Thank God for human monogamy," Saunders concluded.

Ruben Bland did not accomplish his record alone. His first wife bore fifteen children, his second wife nineteen more. He died in 1941, still claiming the title of "champion papa."

If anyone has broken his record, let us know at the North Carolina Collection of the UNC Library, Chapel Hill. Any man who has sired more than thirty-four children deserves recognition, and W.O. Saunders is no longer around to insult him.

The Siamese Twins

CHILDREN BORN WITH THEIR BODIES attached to each other often are called Siamese twins. The reference goes back to Chang and Eng, who took the surname Bunker and became respected citizens of Surry County before dying there 107 years ago.

Born in 1811 of Chinese parents in Siam, Chang and Eng were twin boys physically joined at the breastbone by an "attachment of cartilage and ligaments." Though no doubt there had been other physically joined twins, it was with Chang and Eng that the term "Siamese twins" came into general use to describe that condition.

While in their mid-teens, the boys were discovered in Siam by Robert Hunter, a Scottish merchant who recognized the potential for profit in taking them on tour for public exhibition in Europe and America. In partnership with Abe Coffin, a Massachusetts sea captain, Hunter made a substantial financial arrangement with the boys' parents and also received a release from the king of Siam to remove them from the country. The agreement is sometimes referred to as a "purchase," and indications are that the boys did exist in near-slavery conditions in the years they were associated with Hunter and Coffin.

They first arrived in the United States at Boston in August of 1829, having been insured for $10,000 during the trip. Under various managers, at first Abel Coffin and later others, they set out on tours that usually followed the pattern of renting a room and advertising that they would "receive the public." There was often no admission charge, though pamphlets and lithographs were offered for sale. In addition to touring the United States, they traveled to Europe for extensive tours on three separate occasions. Both in this country and in Europe, the curious came en masse with their money.

For a time in the mid-1830s the twins worked under the direction of the great showman P.T. Barnum—not as part of his circus but as separate "curiosities" exhibited in halls and theaters. Though their relationship with Barnum was not a happy one, the twins came out of retirement from "show business" following the Civil War and again toured under his banner in an attempt to regain some of their lost fortune.

Their residence in North Carolina resulted from an 1837 tour stop in Wilkes County. By that time they already were weary of having people stare at them as freaks, and they wanted to establish a more normal life. Here they found a place they liked and a place where they felt accepted as human beings. Applying for citizenship in 1839, they adopted the last name "Bunker" and opened a "frontier store" in their new Wilkes County home near Traphill. As a means of livelihood the store soon was abandoned in favor of a farm they operated with considerable success.

Most remarkable is that in 1843 the twins married sisters, Sarah and Adelaide Yates, and moved to Surry County. There they built two houses a short distance apart—one for each wife. An arrangement was worked out whereby the twins would spend three days at one house and then three days at the other. The plan is said to have worked out quite well and, in all, twenty-two children were born into the family—twelve by Eng's wife and ten by Chang's wife.

The twins apparently were well accepted by their western North Carolina neighbors, who respected their intelligence and industriousness. Their letter—in which they sometimes refer to themselves as "we" and other times as "I"—indicate that their years in North Carolina were by far the happiest of their lives.

Chang, who previously had suffered a stroke, died in his sleep on January 17, 1874. Eng awoke with a terrible fright and, if a doctor could have arrived in time, no doubt a separation would have been attempted. But within hours, Eng, too, was dead, possibly from fright. An autopsy indicated that an operation to separate the bodies probably would have been unsuccessful.

As they had lived for nearly sixty-three years, the twins were buried as one on the farm. Their bodies were later moved to White Plains Baptist Church.

Charity Bowery,
North Carolina Slave

CHARITY BOWERY WAS LIKE MANY other slaves who had never been permitted to learn to read or write. When she told her story in New York in 1838, she was imprecise about her age and the names of her previous owners. She thought that she was sixty-five; that would have made her birth year about 1773, just before the Revolution. One thing she was sure of: she had lived on a plantation called Pembroke about three miles from Edenton, on North Carolina's Albemarle Sound.

History is the loser because Charity did not record the surname of her first master, for she said that he was a good man who promptly ran off any overseer who mistreated his servants. His mistress, too, was a loving person who treated all slaves with great kindness and who gave each of her children one of Charity's brothers or sisters.

Charity apparently was a favorite in the household, for she was allowed to learn skills that were often limited to the white females—spinning, knitting and weaving. And when Charity married, a preacher performed the ceremony, "for mistress didn't like to have her people take up with one another, without any minister to marry them." Finally, before her death, the master's wife instructed her children that Charity and her husband were never to be separated.

Inherited by a son who got into financial trouble, the couple was, at Charity's suggestion, sold to a man named McKinley (or perhaps McKinsey), "a fine old Christian heart." This new owner soon died, however, and Charity found his widow far less humane. Later it was learned that in his will McKinley had ordered Charity and her husband manumitted—freed from slavery—but the widow refused to divulge the instructions. Charity continued to live in bondage, and her husband died without ever knowing about the provision for freedom.

Intent on earning enough money to buy the freedom of some of her children, the widowed Charity set up an "oyster board" alongside the road near Edenton and in her spare time she sold oysters and crackers to passersby. Among her regular customers was a kind old man who always called her "Aunt Charity." One day, to Charity's surprise and delight, the man purchased her and five of her children from Mrs. McKinley. She was even more thrilled when her new owner announced that he was emancipating Charity and her youngest child, Kitty.

To prevent being re-enslaved, Charity and her child would have to go to the North. Before she left, however, she took all of her savings to her former mistress, Mrs. McKinley, and sought to buy the freedom of her twelve-year-old son, Richard. The widow refused, and instead sold the boy to a speculator. Then Charity offered to buy her little orphan grandson, Sammy. Again Mrs. McKinley refused. So, with a broken heart and her youngest daughter, Charity moved to New York. Free at last, she was haunted by the fact that fifteen of her sixteen children were still in bondage. One of them was so loyal to a wealthy white woman that she was permitted to visit New York with her mistress.

Charity learned that the girl could be emancipated for $400, so the aging freedwoman began taking in washing to earn the necessary money. It is not known if Charity lived long enough to buy the freedom of this daughter, for in 1838 her health was failing. However, we do know that she lived long enough to express her feelings toward her cruel former mistress. Informed that Mrs. McKinley was very ill, Charity sent a message to Edenton: "Tell her to prepare to meet poor Charity at the judgment seat."

Charity Bowery's story was told in 1839 by Lydia Maria Child and published by the American Anti-Slavery Society.

Postmaster Had
Shady Reputation

SARAH DECROW, AMERICA'S FIRST FEMALE postmaster following the adoption
of the federal constitution, was a leading lady in her village of Hertford in
Perquimans County. In fact, she was a versatile woman, and within a year after
her commissioning in 1792, she decided her time was worth more than the income
she was getting from her federal job. Even a letter from the postmaster general's
office informing her that she could keep 40 percent of her receipts (instead of the
20 percent she had been retaining) failed to mollify her.

So Sarah resigned, and on October 1, 1794, Thomas McNider was appointed to
replace her. No figures are available for her tenure, but postal records indicate that
McNider during his first year earned the huge amount of 59 ¢. No wonder Sarah
wanted to get on to other business. Unfortunately, however, she lived only a year or
so, bringing to an end a career that at minimum could be termed colorful.

Not much is known about Sarah's early life, but it is surmised that she was the
daughter of John and Mary Ratlif Moore. She married Ichabod Delano, and they
had at least two children, Mary and Robert. Delano died in 1774, and Sarah then
married Robert Decrow, operator of a local ordinary. Decrow provided Sarah
with a comfortable living, and she helped him run his tavern. He also died in
1784, leaving Sarah with two more young children—Sarah and Elizabeth—and
the ordinary to operate.

Perhaps it was natural for tongues to wag about the widow and her houseguests,
but Sarah went straight to the sheriff when she learned what one Hinchea Gilliam
was saying about her. In her affidavit charging Gilliam with slander, she said that
he had spread the story that "Sarah Decrow is a whore and I can prove that Nat

Williams (meaning a certain Nathaniel Williams who at that time of the speaking the said false, scandalous malicious & opprobrious words Boarded and lodged in the house of the said Sarah) keeps her (meaning the said Sarah and that she lived in a state of Fornication and adultery with the said Nathaniel Williams in open violation of every Law Human and divine)."

It didn't take long for the woman's wrath to win its vengeance, and suddenly Gilliam couldn't remember having uttered the words. Furthermore, he agreed, "if he did use them it was not with any intention of injuring the said Sarah and that he had[n't] any malicious view of hurting the reputation and good fame of the said Sarah, that on the contrary he entertains the highest respect for Mrs. Decrow and has reason to esteem her as a good neighbor." As evidence of her good neighborliness, Sarah accepted his apology and dropped her suit.

Within two years, though, Sarah Moore Delano Decrow was back in court, and this time she was the defendant. Officials charged her with giving service beyond that usually furnished at ordinaries, particularly in regard to the sale of non-tax-paid liquors, a habit that worked to "the great injury of the Revenue of the government."

Sarah's shrewd business sense was demonstrated in still another court case in 1791. One of her lodgers, Dr. Ebenezer Belnap, skipped town without paying his bill. Sarah went to the court and obtained an order attaching the doctor's possessions, which he had carelessly left behind. Among the property that she seized were clothes and personal articles, an assortment of medical supplies and— perhaps most injurious of all to Dr. Belnap—his account book.

If Sarah's public life raised eyebrows among the women of Hertford, it apparently did not sully her reputation among the menfolk who must have recommended her for appointment as the first female postmaster (the title was officially deputy postmaster at the time) following the adoption of federal constitution.

Father, Nine Sons Fight for Confederacy

UNIONIST SENTIMENT DURING THE CIVIL War was strong in western North Carolina, and even some families were divided in their loyalties.

Despite the fact that Stephen Lee had freed his slaves before the war, there was no doubt where every member of his family stood. He and nine of his sons fought for the Confederacy. A native of Charleston, South Carolina, Lee attended the College of Charleston and West Point prior to practicing law. Embarrassed when he won release of a client who was in fact guilty, he took up teaching.

About 1846 Lee moved his family to Buncombe County, where he established a school for boys on a site later occupied by Ambler Sanatorium and eventually a Carmelite Monastery. He constructed a new school in Chunn's Cove and operated it until his death in 1879.

The popular teacher was sixty years old and the father of fourteen or fifteen children when North Carolina seceded from the Union in 1861. He promptly volunteered for duty and earned the distinction of being elected colonel of two different North Carolina regiments—the 15th and 16th. He chose the latter, which at the time was called the 6th Regiment of Volunteers.

Colonel Lee marched his men off to battle in Virginia. During the winter, however, he suffered from chronic diarrhea "attended with a swelling of the legs," and was forced to resign in February. His place was taken by eight of his sons. By February 1865, two months before the war's end, four of these sons were dead of wounds or disease, two were in federal prison camps, one had lost an arm, and only one was still on active duty. A ninth son enlisted a few weeks later.

Unbowed by the impending defeat of the South and the tragedy that had engulfed his family, Colonel Lee, by then almost sixty-four years old and ailing, wrote to President Jefferson Davis about his "ardent desire to contribute to the defense of our beloved country," and requested that he be returned to duty. He formed Lee's Company, called the Silver Greys, of the North Carolina Local Defense Troops. His training of the aging men was so effective that fewer than three hundred of them on April 6, 1865, repulsed a brigade of more than a thousand Union soldiers marching from Tennessee.

Following the Confederate surrender at Appomattox Courthouse and Bennett Place, the five surviving sons, including the one that had lost an arm but had later rejoined his regiment, came home. Colonel Lee returned to teaching and managing his large landholdings that reached from Beaucatcher Mountain to the Swannanoa River. On the recommendation of a neighbor, Samuel C. Shelton, Lee began the cultivation of tobacco, which soon became a principal farm product in Buncombe County.

The Lee School educated many of the area's boys, and according to legend, Beaucatcher Mountain was so named because it was a favorite trysting place for the students and the local girls. Lee died at Asheville on August 2, 1879, honored as the father of nine sons who wore the Confederate gray. He was buried in Riverside Cemetery.

James Iredell Wadell Never Surrendered

IT WAS OVER ONE HUNDRED thirty-five years ago that a Confederate ship captain refused to believe a report in a newspaper that the Civil War had ended. So he kept on attacking Union vessels.

When James Iredell Waddell resigned his commission shortly after the Civil War began, the United States Navy refused to give him his back pay. As an officer in the Confederate Navy three years later, Waddell exacted from the Union an exorbitant interest rate. His price: the destruction of thirty-two Yankee vessels worth more than $1.1 million, plus misery and mortification incapable of being measured in money.

The native of Pittsboro, North Carolina, also compiled the following additional distinctions: he carried in his hip throughout his life a bullet put there by a fellow midshipman whom he had challenged to a duel, he commanded the only Confederate ship to sail around the world during the Civil War, plowing through every major ocean except the Antarctic in his travels of fifty-eight thousand miles and his greatest punishment against the enemy came two months after his native South had surrendered. And, instead of surrendering his ship to the victorious Federal forces, he sailed it to England and walked ashore undefeated.

Named for the Revolutionary patriot and early Supreme Court justice, Waddell was given an appointment to the Naval School when it was located in Norfolk, Virginia. He was later given a commission in the United States Navy and served on several ships before teaching navigation for ten years at the newly established Naval Academy at Annapolis. In that town he married Anna Inglehard.

Lieutenant Waddell had returned to sea when news reached him of the outbreak of the War between the States. Resigning his commission, he slipped through the lines and accepted a commission in the Confederate Navy. After routine assignments for a couple of years, in 1864 Waddell was sent through the blockade to England. There he learned that he had been appointed captain of an English-built ship that had been purchased by the Confederates.

The ship, *Sea King*, was quietly moved to the Madeira Islands where it was converted to a Confederate raider, renamed the *Shenandoah*, and put under Captain Waddell's command. The objective of the *Shenandoah* was to search out and destroy vessels belonging to Northerners, particularly the great whaling fleet in the Pacific. Rounding the Cape of Good Hope, the *Shenandoah* captured and destroyed or bonded several ships before proceeding to Australia for repairs.

From there the ship, under steam or sail as the wind required, turned northward, capturing ships, confiscating supplies and taking prisoners who, from time to time, were placed upon a captured ship to be put ashore at a chosen port. Sailing past Japan, the *Shenandoah* slipped through the Kurile Islands and in the Sea of Okhotsk within sight of Siberia, time and again peacefully approached Northern whalers, ran up the Confederate flag and demanded surrender.

Farther north in the Bering Straits, Captain Waddell spotted a congregation of eleven ships. One had been damaged by an ice floe and ten others had gathered around to see if the captain of the stricken vessel was going to offer bargains before abandoning ship. Waddell sailed the *Shenandoah* into their midst and captured all eleven.

In addition to the thirty-two ships Waddell and his crew scuttled or burned, he bonded six other captured vessels—that is, he required their captains to sign an affidavit committing the spared ships' owners to pay the Confederate government a reward, sometimes $50,000.

On June 23, 1865, the captain of a captured ship showed Waddell a newspaper dated April 17. True, there was a report that Richmond had fallen, but there was also a statement by President Jefferson Davis that the war would continue with vigor. No amount of persuasion by the whalers could convince the Confederate captain that the South had surrendered.

Finally, though, on August 2, while sailing west of California, the *Shenandoah* came upon a British ship whose crew conveyed the unmistakable news that the war had indeed been over since April. Waddell sadly ordered his first lieutenant to "strike below the battery and disarm the ship and crew." The captain, however, chose to avoid the ignominy of surrendering to the government that had cheated him out of his back pay. Instead, he sailed his ship seventeen thousand miles, risking destruction by United States vessels which had been ordered to capture or sink the *Shenandoah*.

On November 6, more than six months after the South surrendered, Waddell sailed his ship into Liverpool, England, dropped anchor, and hauled down the tattered Confederate flag. His account with the United States Navy had been balanced.

Six of Seven Brothers Die in Civil War

Wᴴᴇɴ Jᴏʜɴ W. Bᴏʏʟᴇs ᴀɴᴅ Charity Ferguson were married on June 15, 1831, their future looked bright. They soon accumulated several hundred acres of land in the Mt. Olive section of Stokes County and produced enough tobacco, wheat, corn, flax and other crops to make a comfortable living.

They had eight boys and one girl and they might have lived and died just like thousands of other North Carolina couples, leaving behind a large number of descendants through their nine children. But tragedy was to stalk the Boyles family—the tragedy of the Civil War. When it was over, John and Charity Boyles had lost six sons.

It must have been an inspiring scene at the courthouse in Danbury on March 20, 1862, when four brothers signed enlistment papers to enter the 53rd Regiment of North Carolina Troops. They were John W., Jr., Alexander Martin, James Haywood and Augustin Harmon Boyles.

Not one of them survived the war. John, Jr., died at Petersburg on August 8, 1862, of an unspecified cause; Augustin, according to an army sick report, "contracted fever after a long & fatiguing march" and died October 28, 1862, near Drewry's Bluff; Alexander apparently died from epilepsy and varicose problems shortly after his discharge at Goldsboro on January 30, 1863, and James was killed at Spotsylvania Courthouse in May 1864.

On July 25, 1862, before the loss of any of his brothers, Calvin H. Boyles enlisted in the 21st Regiment at Dansbury. He was wounded near Fredericksburg on May 4, the following year, but returned to duty, only to be killed at Garrett Station, Virginia, on February 11, 1865.

Following the deaths of three brothers in the 53rd Regiment, Irvin Edwin Boyles, age eighteen, sought to fill their places early in 1863. He died of an unspecified disease at Orange Courthouse, Virginia, the following August 10.

Five of his brothers already dead, seventeen-year-old Riley Robertson Boyles joined Calvin in the 21st Regiment on October 15, 1864. Following Calvin's death the following February, Riley wrote his only surviving sibling, Mary Ann: "Dear Sister it is hard times hear [sic]. I have lost six Brothers in this army. I expect to be the next." Ironically, he was the only one of seven brothers in uniform to be spared. An eighth brother, Chaney E. Boyles, was too young to serve.

The names of John and Charity Boyles do not appear in the textbooks, and their contribution of six dead sons in the cause of their state virtually had been forgotten until the late Bell I. Wiley, noted Civil War historian of Emory University, sought to resurrect the tragic story of the Stokes County family.

Wiley wrote: "They are a splendid family and they bear out a feeling based on many years of research that the lowly people were as abundantly endowed with the qualities that count in citizenship as any other class in society."

Blackbeard an Unlickely Ancestor

NOT TOO LONG AGO A woman wanted help from the North Carolina Collection in tracing her ancestry to Edward Teach, better known along the Carolina coast as Blackbeard. We were tempted to ask why, but our job is to pass on information without editorializing. Still, if the meager data available on Blackbeard is accurate, he isn't a very eligible candidate for ancestor worship.

The man called Blackbeard was surrounded by mystery. His real name is not even known; he was variously referred to as Teach, Thatch, Tatch, Tache and Tash. Some writers claim his name was Edward Drummond.

Whether he was born in England or in Virginia, he grew up during the "golden age" of piracy—the late seventeenth and early eighteenth century.

Teach—or whatever his name—first entered history aboard the *Ranger* in the Caribbean. When the *Ranger* captured the French ship, *Concorde*, Teach was allowed to take command of the prize. He changed her name to *Queen Anne's Revenge* and outfitted the vessel as a powerful pirate ship.

Now fully committed to piracy, Teach declined even to spare English ships. He was soon the quarry of the Royal Navy, and he became the most feared pirate afloat. He cultivated a devilish appearance with his long black hair, braided beard, turban-like headdress and belt of pistols and daggers. He seemed to delight in using his nickname, Blackbeard.

It was in 1718 that Blackbeard arrived along the North Carolina coast. Ostensibly he "surrendered" to Governor Charles Eden at Bath under the act of grace by which pirates could be forgiven if they promised not to plunder again. Available evidence, however, seems to indicate that both the governor and Tobias

Knight, secretary of the colony and collector of customs, gave their blessings to the pirate to continue his scourge. With or without such blessings, Blackbeard went on to greater successes.

At the height of his bloody career, he commanded several ships with around four hundred men, and he captured dozens of prizes and dealt mercilessly with their crews. One hideout near Ocracoke Inlet became known as "Blackbeard's Castle" and another as "Teach's Hole."

So powerful was Blackbeard that he demanded and received supplies from the governor and council of South Carolina, and in North Carolina he was a celebrity at Bath where he built a home and, in the presence of the governor, married a sixteen-year-old girl—reputedly his fourteenth wife—whom he forced to submit to both himself and his companions.

Blackbeard's free reign in North Carolina was not appreciated by Virginia shippers whose crew grew increasingly reluctant to go to sea. Virginia Governor Spotswood determined to track down and get rid of the menace of the sea. He outfitted two sloops that in November 1718, engaged Blackbeard's ship, the *Adventure*, in Ocracoke Inlet.

After an inconclusive exchange of gunfire, Lieutenant Robert Maynard brought his sloop alongside the pirate ship, and the crews turned to hand-to-hand fighting. In heroic style, Maynard and Blackbeard squared off in a fearsome clash of cutlasses that left the pirate dead with twenty-five wounds. His head was severed and swung beneath the bowsprit of the victorious sloop.

In Bath, Governor Eden and Secretary Knight laid claim to the pirate's goods. Even the Lords Proprietors of Carolina entered a claim, and it was not until after a vice-admiralty court ruling that the plunder was finally distributed to the victorious Virginians who had defeated Blackbeard.

In addition to what booty they had already shared during Blackbeard's brief but lucrative harvest off North Carolina, Eden and Knight earned a lasting reputation for having consorted with pirates.

Hanging of
Calvin and Thomas Coley

C AL HAD CEASED HIS STRUGGLE, but Tom's body was still swaying several minutes after the double hanging, and Dr. O.L. Ellis waited behind his big camera to get a perfect picture of the dramatic scene.

Impatient, the physician, justice of the peace and amateur photographer persuaded a member of the Franklin Guards to grab the dead man's left leg to steady the swinging body. Another young guardsman stood with his sword pointing upward.

In the background the camera captured the elaborate platform whose neatly hinged front edges had been sprung, carrying the Coley brothers to their deaths. Eight empty chairs were arranged in a disorderly fashion, witness to the speed with which their occupants had left the stage.

Visible, too, was the rope around Cal's neck. This was no ordinary rope; it was, one might say, a ceremonial rope, noted for its efficiency. In fact, Cal's rope, generously loaned to Franklin County by Sheriff W.M. Page of Wake County, had been used previously on Henry Jones and J.C. Parrish of Wake, William Bostick of Moore and Charles Blackburn and Charles Reynolds of Guilford County. Furthermore, it was already "booked up" for the next month—once in Alamance and once in Wake. It is not clear why Cal rather than Tom was accorded the privilege of being executed by the famous hanging rope.

Dr. Ellis's photograph, now darkened by age, provides the frontispiece for a new book, *The Day the Black Rain Fell*, written and published by William F. Shelton of Louisburg, North Carolina. It took ten years of research for Shelton to uncover the story of how and why Calvin and Thomas Coley came to be hanged at Louisburg on July 13, 1894. The title of the book alludes to the "black rain" that old-timers claim fell on Franklin County the day of the hangings.

The story begins in 1892 when Samuel Tucker, a twenty-five-year-old Russian Jew, peddled his cart of dry goods and trinkets from farm to farm in Franklin County. As night approached that summer, Tucker sought supper and lodging at the home of N.C. Gupton in Gold Mine Township. His own house was full of children, so Gupton was unable to accommodate the engaging young peddler. Instead, he recommended the next house, occupied by two women known locally as Lucy Brewer and Pinkey Wilkins. However, Gupton cautioned Tucker that the women sometimes had as callers hard-drinking brothers by the name of Cal and Tom Coley.

The young Jew could hardly be choosy in rural Franklin County, so he asked for and was rented a room for the night by the women. For a year and a half nothing more was seen of the Russian peddler, and residents assumed that he had left the county.

On Christmas Eve of 1893, however, Lit Wester and Irving King stumbled upon a skeleton near the women's home while turkey hunting. At first, authorities thought the skeleton was that of Cal Coley, who with Pinkey had not been seen recently. When questioned, however, Lucy confessed that on that July night the previous year Cal and Tom had murdered the Jewish peddler with an axe. His body had been thrown into a ravine and his money and goods shared by the quartet. Tom was found near the Portis Gold Mine, and Cal and Pinkey were extradited from Norfolk, Virginia.

In January 1894 the brothers were convicted and sentenced to be hanged. In the following weeks, a Baptist minister, the Reverend W.B. Morton, patiently visited the prisoners and sought their conversion. One day, as the jailer admitted the minister to their cell, Cal and Tom attacked them and rushed from the jail, only to be caught before getting out of town.

Thousands gathered on the dark July day and watched as the Coley brothers were hanged and Dr. Ellis got his picture. The bodies were placed in pine coffins and taken eastward by wagon. Near Wood's Store the box holding Cal's body was bumped off the wagon. It fell in the muddy road and split open.

Finally, the coffins reached a cemetery in Nash County, and there Cal and Tom were buried beside another brother who himself had been a murder victim.

Martha McFarlane McGee Bell, Heroine

WHEN COLONEL JOHN MCGEE DIED in 1774 at his home on Sandy Creek in Orange (later Guilford, now Randolph) County just south of the present town of Julian, he left a hardy wife to care for his ordinary, store, mill and other substantial property holdings.

The former officer in the British army had done well since coming to the frontier and taking as his wife a neighbor named Martha McFarlane. Martha bore him five more children to go with the two that McGee already had from a previous marriage. Martha was noted in the community for helping others, often serving as a midwife and nurse. She also worked beside McGee in directing his business affairs, so she was not entirely inexperienced when his death placed heavy responsibilities on her shoulders.

For six years she valiantly carried on the business while rearing the children. As the most eligible widow in the county, she bided her time as suitors called. Finally, in 1779 she married William Bell, who operated similar business interests at the junction of Muddy Creek and Deep River, just northwest of the present town of Randleman.

Whatever his other attractions, William Bell shared Martha's enthusiastic support of the American forces fighting the British and Tories. Bell, in fact, was one of the most prominent Patriots of the area. He helped organize Randolph County in 1779 and was its first sheriff. For several years the county court met at his "former" dwelling house, and he served three terms in the House of Commons.

He was also a commissary, providing provisions to the American forces. This made him a target of the Tories in the backcountry, and he took refuge with the militia for months at a time, leaving Martha to run the mill and farm.

His absence also opened the way for Martha to become a heroine. The iron-willed businesswoman often joined the male Patriots who met at Bell Mill. She was not averse to carrying arms, and Tory marauders on more than one occasion barely escaped when they tried to plunder her plantation. It was immediately after the battle of Guilford Courthouse, however, that Martha won her lasting recognition.

British General Cornwallis marched his barely victorious army southeasterly. He confronted Martha McFarlane McGee Bell and asked for the use of her home, plantation and mill for two days while his troops rested and regained strength. Noting that the general had the power to commandeer her property with or without her permission, she had a simple question: would he burn her mill after it had served his purpose?

Cornwallis pledged that no harm would be done to the mill, but asked why the question. Martha replied that had he not given his pledge, she would have burned her own mill before it could be put to his benefit. Two days later Cornwallis marched his forces away. He had kept his promise. Very soon, an American force arrived at Bell's Mill. These pursuing Patriots wondered where Cornwallis might make his next camp. They planned a sneak attack.

Martha volunteered to find out. She mounted her horse and rode hard, catching up with the British at Walker's Mill. She boldly rode into camp, demanding to see General Cornwallis, to whom she complained that the British had committed damage to her property that she had not observed until after he left. Affecting outrage for not having received satisfaction, Martha rode around the camp, carefully observing the placement of various units. This information, carried back to the Americans, enabled them successfully to attack the British.

During the remainder of the war, Tory bands, such as one led by Colonel David Fanning, repeatedly raided the Bell property, but they failed to burn it. Martha's reputation as a heroine grew.

Both Martha and William lived into their eighties. She died in September 1820, and William died the following October. The *Raleigh Register* described him as a "firm patriot in our Revolutionary struggle." Both were buried in the Bell-Welborn cemetery in Randolph.

More than a century later, the DAR erected a monument to Martha Bell at Guilford Battleground. She is described as "Loyal Whig, Enthusiastic Patriot, Revolutionary Heroine."

The Story of a Runaway

Early on a chilly morning in October 1866, a Burke County youngster was instructed by his father to fetch wood and build a fire. Instead, the seventeen-year-old stuffed his pockets with bread and sweet potatoes, threw over his shoulder a pillowcase full of clothing and left home. When he returned a decade later, he picked up an armful of wood and toted it into the house. At last, he had carried out his father's orders.

And in those absent ten years, the young man had accomplished his dream of obtaining an education and returning to serve his fellow mountaineers. It was, after all, the father's lack of interest in educating his son that drove Robert Logan Patton from home with less than a dollar in his pocket on that cold morning shortly after the end of the Civil War.

Now he was back home, and the story of his struggle for an education stirred western North Carolina for generations. It was from a prostrate state that young Patton fled in 1866. For weeks he walked across the mountains, sleeping in the woods, offering to do chores in return for an occasional meal, always fearful that someone would divulge his whereabouts to his father.

He was in Jonesboro, Tennessee, working as a railroad hand to earn money to attend Jonesboro Academy, when he learned that his father had traced him and was coming for him. So Robert Logan Patton resumed his walking through Cumberland Gap into Kentucky. Again he worked with the railroad at Crab Orchard, then set out for Indiana, looking for a community with an academy which he could attend while working for his keep and tuition.

In Indiana he hired himself out to one John Ulmer, who agreed to pay him for working on dry days and to allow him to study on rainy days. This employment ended when a brother, John Sidney Patton, caught up with him. The two set out for Illinois, again sleeping wherever they could find shelter and often subsisting on parched corn.

At Neoga, Illinois, a neighbor from Burke County, James F. Spainhour, joined the brothers. They pooled their resources, bought a long-handled frying pan and a mess of bacon and meal, and headed for Kansas, where well-paying jobs were reported to be available.

At Hillsboro, Illinois, however, the Patton brothers changed their minds, and they let Spainhour proceed to Kansas alone. What attracted the boys was Hillsboro Academy and the opportunity to work their way through school. Although neither had been exposed to more than rudimentary schooling, they were given jobs teaching in a local public school. For the remainder of each year, they spent their earnings as students in the academy. Logan also for two years rang the bell, made the fires and swept out the academy building.

After finishing a three-year course at Hillsboro Academy, Robert L. Patton borrowed $40 from a Presbyterian Church elder and followed his brother to Phillips Exeter Academy in Massachusetts. There the brothers performed a variety of jobs in exchange for tuition, room and board. Logan daily swept out a five-story building, made up twenty beds, waited on tables and started the fires. When he finished the course in 1872, he was out of debt.

His brother went on to Harvard, but the younger Patton worked on a farm in Massachusetts and in the fall entered Amherst College. He was the first Southerner to enroll there after the war, a distinction that worked to his advantage. He was given an overcoat, a suit of clothes and other kindnesses were shown him by students and faculty. One lady painted him a Confederate flag for his room.

But his struggle for enough money to pay his tuition and other expenses continued, and he later wrote, "My principal food was molasses, baker's bread, and cracked wheat, which like rice I cooked on my little coal stove."

With scholarships, several part-time jobs and assistance from the Baptist Education Board, Robert Logan Patton graduated from Amherst College in 1876. After a full decade, he was ready to return home and carry in the load of wood that he had been sent for in 1866.

Was Nellie Cropsey Murdered?

WHEN ON DECEMBER 4, 1934, James E. Wilcox shot himself in Elizabeth City, the secret of the disappearance and death of Nellie Cropsey was sealed forever. A third of a century had passed since Nellie's body was found floating in the Pasquotank River. Nearly all fingers pointed to her former lover, who barely escaped lynching and was twice convicted of her murder.

Nellie—her real name was Ella Maude—grew up in Brooklyn, New York, and moved to Elizabeth City in 1898 with her parents and four sisters, Ollie, Lettie, Mamie and Lou. Of the young Tar Heels who sought Nellie's attention, Jim Wilcox was her favorite. Their courtship, however, was punctuated by occasional lovers' spats, and when a Brooklyn cousin, Carrie, came to visit in 1901, Nellie sulked over Jim's attention to the visitor.

In fact, Jim was friendly with all the girls. On that night of November 20, 1901, however, Nellie sat quietly mending a coat as Jim Wilcox and Roy Crawford chatted in the Cropsey living room with Ollie and Carrie. Only reluctantly was Nellie drawn into the conversation when the subject of dying came up. She said if she had to die, she would rather freeze to death.

It was about eleven o'clock when Jim rolled a cigarette, got his hat and prepared to leave. In the hall he called to Nellie, asking if he could see her a minute. Nellie Cropsey put down her mending and went to the door with him. A half hour later when Roy left, Ollie was puzzled by the open front door.

Ollie went to bed, waiting for Nellie to join her. Shortly after the 12:30 whistle blew, barking dogs near the pigpen led her father downstairs with his gun. Ollie got up and cautioned him not to shoot blindly, for Nellie and Jim were out in the yard.

Another hour passed, and Nellie had not returned. Alarmed, the family called the sheriff, who immediately went to the Wilcox home to see if Jim had returned. Found in bed, Jim was hustled off to the Cropsey home. He reported that he had left Nellie crying on the front porch after he told her that their courtship was over.

The mystery of Nellie's whereabouts lasted for thirty-seven days. Widespread suspicion that she either committed suicide or had been murdered was confirmed when her body floated to the surface of the river within sight of the home from which she had walked or was dragged that November night.

An autopsy ruled that she died from a blow to the head rather than from drowning, and the jailed Jim Wilcox was on several occasions threatened by an angry mob. In superior court, he was convicted, on circumstantial evidence, of first-degree murder and sentenced by Judge George A. Jones to "hang by the neck until dead." The state supreme court, however, overturned the conviction on the grounds that the defendant's rights were abridged by the incendiary mood of the town.

Retried in Perquimans County in 1903, Wilcox was found guilty of second-degree murder and given a thirty-year sentence. Still contending he was innocent, Jim Wilcox became a model prisoner. On December 20, 1918, after a personal conference with the prisoner, Governor Thomas W. Bickett pardoned him.

Back in Elizabeth City, Wilcox found himself something of an outcast. He could not find a good job, and people shunned him. At the Baptist Church, two parishioners got up and moved across the aisle from him. The fire department, however, gave him a place to sleep in return for his keeping the engines shined and tuned.

In the early 1930s, Wilcox worked for a time with a commercial fisherman at Nags Head. While there he stayed up nights writing what he claimed to be the full story of his relations with Nellie Cropsey. He sealed the document in a waterproof box and sank it in a shallow part of the sound, the spot marked by a stake. If anything should happen to him, he told a fellow fisherman, the box should be retrieved and the contents released to the press.

Wilcox moved back to Elizabeth City, stole a shotgun, lay down on a cot in a hovel-like room furnished by a friend, and ended the life that the state twice had failed to claim. Shortly before, a hurricane swept away Wilcox's stake, and the box was never recovered. Thus Jim Wilcox took his secret to the grave.

North Carolinian Held Weight Record

To say that Miles Darden lived an obscure life would be an exaggeration, for he was much in evidence wherever he went. After all, he weighed over half a ton and for a century held the record as the world's heaviest human being.

Strangely, though, not much is known about the background of Miles (sometimes spelled Mills) Darden. Tradition has it that he was born in 1798 on a farm near Rich Square in Northampton County, North Carolina, but another source claims he was born at Salisbury. It is agreed, however, that as a youth he moved to Southampton County, Virginia, and thence to Henderson County, Tennessee.

In Tennessee, Darden farmed and led a normal life for many years. He was very popular among his neighbors. Heavy even as a child, he continued to add weight, and in 1839 a tailor in Lexington, Tennessee, made a new coat for him. To test its size, three men, each weighing over two hundred pounds, buttoned it around themselves and walked around the square in Lexington.

By 1845 Darden weighed over eight hundred fifty pounds, and his height was given variously as seven feet six inches and seven feet nine inches. Soon he required over thirteen yards of cloth for a coat, and he wore a size eight and a half hat.

Until he was forty-five, Darden was able to work in the fields, but after that time he stayed home occasionally being carried for a ride on a two-horse wagon. Before the rolls of fat closed his windpipe and killed him on January 23, 1857, Darden had reached the astounding weight of one thousand twenty pounds.

A special coffin was built for him. It measured more than eight feet long, thirty-five inches deep, thirty-two inches across the breast, eighteen inches across the head and fourteen inches at the feet. It was covered with twenty-five yards of black velvet. His body was buried at Chapel Hill Church near Lexington, Tennessee, and subsequently the community in which he lived was named Darden in his honor.

Miles Darden's record as the heaviest man was from time to time challenged, but proof was absent until 1958 when Robert Earl Hughes of Monticello, Illinois, weighed in at one thousand sixty-nine pounds. His waist was one hundred twenty-two inches, chest one hundred twenty-four inches and upper arm forty inches. Later that year Hughes died, taking with him the world record, now recognized by the *Guinness Book of Records*.

Miles (or Mills) Darden, however, holds onto second place, according to Guinness. Furthermore, the North Carolina native retains another interesting record: the greatest weight differential between a man and his wife. Since Darden's wife Nancy weighed only ninety-eight pounds, the differential was nine hundred twenty-two pounds! Despite this differential, Mrs. Darden bore her husband three children before her death in 1837.

North Carolina holds another record for heaviness: Billy and Benny McCrary (alias Bill and Benny McGuire), born in 1948 at Hendersonville, were the heaviest twins on record. In 1970 they weighed six hundred sixty and six hundred forty pounds, respectively, and after they became professional wrestlers, they were billed at weights of up to seven hundred seventy pounds apiece. Billy died in 1979.

There appears to be no scientific explanation for the obesity records of North Carolinians. Maybe it is because we have good water, good food and good atmosphere, and that we have a weakness for all three.

Phineas T. Barnum in North Carolina

P HINEAS T. BARNUM WAS A loveable humbug. Or, at least, he was a master at
making a silk purse from a sow's ear.

Take, for instance, his autobiographical claim that on October 30, 1836, at
Warrenton, North Carolina, he departed on good terms with his partner, Aaron
Turner, and began his own company. The circus had been performing during
Warrenton's annual fall races.

Barnum wrote, "I now separated from the circus company, taking Vivalla,
James Sanford (a Negro singer and dancer), several musicians, horses, wagons,
and a small canvas tent with which I intended to begin a traveling exhibition of my
own." Turner, wrote Barnum, "wished me every success in my new venture."

The fact is that three weeks later in Raleigh the two troupes competed for the
same audience. One featured "Signor Vivalla, the celebrated Italian Professor
of Equilibrium and Plate Dancing," described as the wonder of the world, and
"Mr. Sanford from the New York Theaters." This show was performed in the old
museum, near Carter's Hotel. The price was 50¢ for adults, 25¢ for children and
servants.

Simultaneously, at the music pavilion was performing the "unparalleled
attraction—the Old Colombian Circus, under the direction of A. Turner and
Co." Its admission price was only 25¢ for adults, half of that for children and
slaves. His former partner thus undercut the upstart Barnum.

P.T. Barnum's name did not appear in the press. His role, one discovers by
perusing his autobiography, was really that of advertising the Vivalla show, selling
tickets and on stage, handing the magician a pistol, which he discharged while

"dancing" ten plates at one time.

It was in Raleigh, if we are to believe Barnum, that he sold a half interest in his struggling troupe to a man called Henry. Later, in Augusta, Georgia, the sheriff sought to foreclose on the circus property to satisfy Henry's debts. Barnum wrote proudly of his shrewdness in outwitting both the law and Henry and regaining sole ownership of the company.

Barnum's skill as a humbug had thus been highly developed by the time he was twenty-six years of age. He had served a term in prison for libel during his brief tenure as an editor, and he had held a variety of jobs—among them bartender, storekeeper, grocer and ticket taker at a theater.

He started his own show business by buying Joice Heth, a slave alleged to be one hundred sixty-one years old, one hundred sixteen years of which had been spent as a devout Baptist. Armed with fake documents purporting to prove that the woman had been little George Washington's nurse, Barnum exhibited Joice until she died—one assumes from being worn out.

When an autopsy revealed that the dead woman was only about eighty years old, Barnum peddled news stories, accusing her former owner of misrepresentation. He himself claimed complete innocence.

Barnum joined Turner only a few months before they parted company in Warrenton. After completing a southern tour, he bought out two exhibition houses and formed his popular "American Museum" in New York City.

A master at promotion, the showman drew worldwide attention when he traveled in Europe in 1844 with the dwarf, "General Tom Thumb," (actually Charles Sherwood Stratton). In 1850, almost entirely on brass and nerve, Barnum brought Jenny Lind to the United States. She in turn brought him additional fame and fortune.

In his native Connecticut after the Civil War, Barnum served in the state legislature and lost a race for congress. In 1881 he joined James A. Bailey in forming the Barnum and Bailey Circus, touted as "The Greatest Show on Earth."

Barnum's most remembered appearance in North Carolina occurred near Rocky Mount two weeks after his split-up with Turner in 1836. As he approached the Falls of the Tar Baptist Church, he came upon an outdoor service.

The brassy Yankee waited until the preacher had finished, then for nearly an hour he addressed the three hundred people, warning them that "diamonds may glitter on a vicious breast." Undoubtedly he took the occasion to remind the Tar Heels that his troupe would be performing that evening in a tent nearby.

When he died in 1891, Barnum left behind a famous quotation: "A sucker is born every minute." Few who were duped by him, however, held a grudge against the lovable humbug and talented showman.

L.A. Scruggs, North Carolina's First Black Doctor

Hᴉsᴛᴏʀʏ ᴡᴀs ᴍᴀᴅᴇ ɪɴ Nᴏʀᴛʜ Carolina when on May 18, 1886, the North Carolina Board of Medical Examiners licensed forty-six men to practice in North Carolina.

Of special significance were the last three names on the list: M.T. Pope of Rich Square, L.A. Scruggs of Liberty, Virginia, and J.T. Williams of Charlotte. Each of the three names was accompanied by the designation "col'd."

The development was reported in the North Carolina Medical Journal: "We note with much satisfaction that among the licentiates of the Board of Examiners at New Bern there were three colored men, all of whom, we are informed, where well worthy of the official permission to practice medicine and surgery which they received at the hands of the Examiners."

The editor of the journal, Dr. Thomas F. Wood, exhibited some nervousness over the history-making licensing of three black physicians. They would, he wrote, "do much for the elevation of the character of their colored friends, as well as enlighten their minds in purifying their life and thoughts," provided the new doctors carried out their responsibilities without the "vain-glorious parade of their knowledge."

Of these three who were licensed, it was Lawson Andrew Scruggs who became best known in his adopted state. Born to slaves in Bedford County, Virginia, in 1857, the boy grew up on a tenant farm. Little schooling was available for Negroes, but the youngster learned to read and write well enough to become the unofficial letter writer for illiterate playmates.

Anxious to get away from the farm, the young man joined a labor gang to work on telegraph lines in the South. At age twenty, he entered Richmond Institute, operated by the Baptist Home Mission Society. He graduated five years later.

A whole new world opened to the student, whose potential was quickly recognized by school officials. That fall Scruggs entered Shaw Institute in Raleigh, and he received a literary degree in 1885 and a medical degree the following year. He was valedictorian of both classes.

After passing the medical examination and obtaining his license, Dr. Scruggs was employed by Shaw as resident physician and instructor of hygiene and physiology. More importantly, he was appointed a resident physician at Leonard Hospital, operated in connection with the medical school. He was also a registered pharmacist.

For a time Dr. Scruggs was first medical lecturer and visiting physician at St. Augustine's Normal and Collegiate Institute, and when St. Agnes Hospital was opened in 1896, he became its only black staff doctor. All the while he carried on a substantial private practice among Raleigh's blacks, caring for as many as two thousand patients per year.

In 1897 Scruggs organized the Old North State Medical, Dental and Pharmaceutical Association, and the capital city's chapter was named the L.A. Scruggs Medical Society. The physician was also active in religious and cultural affairs, serving as state correspondent of the National Baptist. And in 1892, he published a rather remarkable book, *Women of Distinction*, containing biographies of black American women "remarkable in works and invincible in character."

Other blacks may have practiced medicine earlier in North Carolina (presumably by being licensed in northern states) but Lawson A. Scruggs was the first to be licensed by the North Carolina board and to make a name for himself in the practice of medicine in the Old North State.

Major George E. Preddy, Jr., Flying Ace

W HEN MAJOR GEORGE EARL PREDDY, Jr., returned to Greensboro in September 1944, he was received as the hero that he was—a flyer who had broken Captain Eddy Rickenbacker's World War I record for enemy planes shot down.

The major could have returned home many months earlier after he finished his first two hundred hours of combat, but he had repeatedly asked for extensions of duty. Now, after an exciting summer, he took advantage of a short respite from the war.

Before leaving Europe he was featured on CBS in an interview by Bill Shadel beamed all over the world. The program was introduced by Edward R. Murrow, who had been born only a few miles from Preddy's home in Guilford County. Thus Americans were acquainted with the exploits of George Preddy. In the nation's capital he was caught up in a whirl of interviews and public appearances.

George Preddy, Jr., was born in Greensboro on February 5, 1919. After attending Guilford College, he fell in love with flying. In 1941 he joined the Army Air Corps.

Early in the war he was sent to Australia from where he flew about two dozen missions against the Japanese. On a training mission his plane collided with that of another American, and Preddy parachuted into the jungle. He was eventually rescued.

In 1943 Preddy was returned to the United States, then sent to England. On December 1, while escorting American bombers over Germany, he scored his first hit on a Nazi plane. Two days later he scored another, and he was decorated with a Silver Star.

The danger of combat flying was rudely brought home to George Preddy on January 29, 1944, when his P-47 was hit by flak over the English Channel. He bailed out and was soon plucked out of the water. In the spring Preddy's toll of enemy planes was mounting, and he was made commander of the 487th Fighter Squadron of P-51 Mustangs. On D-Day he and his squadron attacked ground transportation and installations.

July was a splendid month, then came August 6. Major Preddy and his squadron were escorting B-17 bombers over Hamburg when more than thirty German planes attacked. By the time the skirmish was over, the camera in Preddy's Mustang, *Cripes A'Mighty*, had recorded the awesome toll. He had shot down six Nazi aircraft, a record for the European theatre. That brought his record to twenty-nine enemy planes destroyed, and he was awarded the Distinguished Service Cross, the nation's second highest military honor.

It was at this point that he came home to a hero's welcome. While in the states, he visited his brother, William R. Preddy, who was in air force training in Florida. By special permission they were allowed to put on an air duel, and the ace was much impressed by his brother's developing skill.

By November Major Preddy was back in Europe; he was made commander of the 328th Fighter Squadron which moved its base to Belgium.

Christmas Day was just another day of war, and George Peddy led his squadron on a mission to Coblenz. He shot down two German planes and headed back. Near the Belgian border they encountered several more "bandits." His wingman described what happened; Preddy began chasing Nazi craft at low altitude. Suddenly they were over friendly ground antiaircraft fire, and before Preddy could pull out of his maneuver, his plane was hit. "I saw no chute and watched his ship hit," his colleague wrote.

Upon learning of his brother's death, Bill wrote his parents from England, "Let us carry on as George wanted and may we survive at his standard." Shortly afterward, Lieutenant Bill Preddy shot down two German planes. Then, three months later, he went down with his plane near Prague, Czechoslovakia.

In the American cemetery at St. Avold, France, stand two white crosses side by side. One reads "George E. Preddy, Jr.," and the other bears the inscription, "William R. Preddy."

Aunt Abby House Was "True Grit"

Aunt Abby House was liberated long before the term took on its current meaning. Pity the person who crossed her, particularly if he wore a blue uniform. She took guff from nobody, least of all a Yankee or a Republican.

In fact, she was a downright cantankerous old biddy. She had a habit of barging right in on the menfolks' meetings, and nobody dared kick her out. She became the first woman to vote in a political convention in North Carolina. When the Democrats met to select a candidate for the governorship in 1876, Aunt Abby marched in to see that things went right. Paul C. Cameron sized up the situation and decided that the convention would be more peaceful with her present than by trying to get rid of her. So he called her up to sit by him.

Zeb Vance, Aunt Abby's idol, was nominated for governor, and as the voting began, someone observed that Clay County was not represented. By unanimous consent, Abby House was permitted to cast Clay's vote—for Vance, of course. [Zebulon Vance was previously North Carolina's governor during the Civil War.]

At Vance's inaugural, Aunt Abby was right there. When he ended his oath with "I will, so help me God," she echoed, "That you will, honey, that you will."

About that time an artist, Willis Holt Fergurson, drew a cartoon. "The Burial of Radicalism," which shows Aunt Abby raising her hands in victory and saying "Zeb, you're setting Carolina free makes me feel like a gal again."

It must have been a mighty good feeling, for Aunt Abby had lived a long time since her childhood.

Born in Franklin County in 1797, Abby House watched her boyfriend go off to the army in the War of 1812. Hearing that he was ill, she walked all the way to

Norfolk only to find that he had been buried. For the next half century she farmed in Franklin County. Although she lived simply, she acquired a substantial amount of property.

Then came the Civil War, and Franklin County's young men went off to battle, including Abby House's nephews whom she loved as if they were her own children.

One of them was reported ill, and Abby went to Virginia to look after him. Soon she became a sort of nurse and courier, going to and from the battlefields, cooking, taking care of the sick and carrying clothing and food to the soldiers.

By the hundreds, soldiers came to know Aunt Abby, a familiar figure on the Raleigh and Gaston Railroad and in the Confederate lines. As an angel of mercy, she never thought of paying a fare and if she had trouble getting through the lines, she would demand to see the highest officer, state her business and then proceed.

When Jefferson Davis was on his last retreat, Aunt Abby met his procession in Greensboro and cooked him a meal. She later reported that the president said, "Goodbye, Aunt Abby. You are true grit, but it is just what I expected of you."

After the war Aunt Abby had a hard time. She lost most of her land, and her health began to fail. Hearing of her condition, a group of admirers of the "Florence Nightingale of North Carolina" bought a little cottage for her near the present site of Raleigh's Little Theatre. There she spent her last years.

One of her last public appearances was in 1879 at Louisburg's centennial celebration. As the parade was about to begin, Aunt Abby walked up to Vance's carriage and climbed aboard, shocking only those too young to know the legendary woman.

Her health failed rapidly after that, and this "venerable woman," as *The News and Observer* called her, died on November 23, 1881. The newspaper added that Abby House was "cast in a Roman mould, and was strong in her likes and dislikes."

She was buried in the Dickerson Family cemetery at Franklinton. A marker reads, "Aunt Abby House, Angel of Mercy to the Confederate Soldiers."

Tiny Broadwicke, Pioneer Aviatrix

Perhaps it was just one of the signs of the times; the world seemed too busy celebrating the first successful manned balloon flight across the Atlantic to pay much attention to the death of aviation's pioneer woman parachutist.

Ben Abruzzo, Maxie Anderson and Larry Newman are the heroes of the moment, whereas Tiny Broadwicke's exploits took place over a half-century ago. Still, her death in California deserves notice, particularly by her fellow North Carolinians.

She was really Mrs. Georgia Thompson Brown, but the public knew her as Tiny Broadwicke—the first word describing her size, the second representing the name of the man who made her famous. Born Georgia Ann Thompson on a farm near Henderson, North Carolina, in 1893, the youngster was already a widow and mother when in 1908 at the age of fifteen she visited the state fair. There she watched intently as a carnival balloonist prepared his contraption for ascent.

She later said, "When I saw that balloon go up and I gawked at it as it ascended into the heavens, I knew I'd never be the same." She pestered the balloonist to give her a ride. Impressed by her gall and her size—four foot eight inches and less than one hundred pounds—Charles Broadwicke, the balloonist, allowed himself to be talked into making her a part of his act. In fact, she took his name, and as Tiny Broadwicke, the Doll Girl, she was to make aviation history.

For several years the act traveled with the Johnny J. Jones Carnival. Tiny said: "I toured the country with the carnival, making as many as three cutaways in one jump. A cutaway is when you release one chute and open another. I dropped in one chute from the balloon, then slipped out of that one into another and out of that one into still another before hitting the ground."

Charles Broadwicke developed for Tiny a special type of backpack parachute, and in 1912 a young man named Glenn L. Martin watched her act with great interest. Martin, whose name was to become familiar in aviation, believed that airplane pilots should be prepared to use parachutes, and he sought to prove his point. On June 21, 1913, he carried aloft Tiny Broadwicke who parachuted into Griffith Park, Los Angeles—the first woman ever to jump from an airplane. Later the same year Martin flew her in a seaplane, and Tiny parachuted into Lake Michigan.

In 1914 Tiny conducted a series of jumps in the "Coatpack" developed by Charles. These demonstrations finally convinced the army of the practicability of providing parachutes for airplane pilots.

For the next two years Tiny was an exhibition parachute jumper at the San Diego World's Fair. She continued jumping until 1922 when she estimated her total number of descents at over a thousand.

Her last jump was a memorable one. The Curtis Jenny Biplane was piloted by another famed aviator, Clyde Pangborne, and the mayor of Los Angeles was on hand to observe.

Commenting on her many experiences, Tiny said: "Oh, I got banged up all right. Broken bones. Sprained ankles. Wrenched back. Dislocated shoulder. But I was young and loved every minute." She continued, "Sometimes I wound up tangled in tree limbs. Sometimes I splashed into rivers, lakes and mud ponds. Once I landed in high voltage wires." And another time she fell onto a caboose of a freight train pulling out of a station.

Tiny Broadwicke became a legend among aviators. She was the last surviving female member of the Early Birds, an organization of persons who soloed prior to December 19, 1916. When someone questioned her qualifications for membership, she quipped, "Well, I went up in the balloon and nobody brought me down."

Tiny Broadwicke remained a darling of aviators through her life, and she was frequently the person of honor at air shows and demonstrations. One of her historic parachutes is preserved in the North Carolina Division of Archives and History, another in the Smithsonian Institution.

Tiny was brought back for burial in her native Vance County, from where years ago she left her twelve-hour-per-day cotton mill job for the excitement of the sky. Her name will live in the annals of aviation history.

New Hanover Slave Finally Escapes

W HEN THOMAS H. JONES DICTATED his story in Boston in 1849, he had been a fugitive only three months. His first wife and four of his children remained in slavery in North Carolina.

Thomas was born about 1806 on a plantation owned by John Hawes between the Black and South Rivers in New Hanover County. For nine years he lived with his parents in a clay-floor log slave cabin with a mud and stick chimney.

Hawes, according to Thomas, was a "severe and cruel master" who with the aid of his sons, Enoch, Edward and John, managed his plantation without an overseer. About 1815 Hawes sold Thomas to a Mr. Jones of Wilmington. Assigned to tasks around the house—carrying wood, building fires and fetching water—the youngster was later made a cook.

Finally, he was made a handyman in Jones's store where the clerk, David Cogdell, was exceptionally good to him. Years later Thomas spoke fondly of Cogdell's "generous treatment and noble kindness to a despised and unhappy boy."

When Cogdell was dismissed, James Dixon, a boy of Thomas's age, was made clerk. Dixon spent part of the day studying. The young slave became fascinated with the clerk's books and asked to see his spelling book.

The combination of pictures and words made little sense to Thomas, but he secretly vowed to learn to read and write, in defiance of custom. He managed to obtain a spelling book and, for 6¢ a week, persuaded a white boy, Hiram Brecket, to spend a few minutes per day instructing him.

He hid his book among barrels of liquor in the store, and he kept a pencil under his bed in his cabin. Then one evening by candlelight, after many trials, he finally printed the words "THOMAS JONES." It was a proud moment, but he could share it with no one.

His pride in his accomplishment, however, opened a whole new world for Thomas Jones. He began associating with free blacks such as James Galley, Jack Cammon and Binney Pennison, who were active in the Methodist Church. Jones objected strongly to his slave's meddling with religion, and Thomas endured several severe beatings until his owner, apparently mellowing because of the influence of his wife, finally gave him a "paper" allowing him to join the church.

When Thomas was twenty-two years old, he was sold to Owen Holmes for $435. It was at this time that Thomas, for the first time in thirteen years, was allowed to visit his mother at the Hawes plantation. He found that his father, brother and sister had been sold away and that his mother was "old, heartbroke, utterly desolate, weak and dying alone."

Back in Wilmington, Thomas took as his common-law wife Lucilla Smith, a seamstress belonging to a Mrs. Moore. They had three children. Then Mrs. Moore moved away and took Lucilla and the children with her.

Alone again, Thomas paid his master $150 per year in order to be able to hire himself out as a stevedore. He made a dollar or more a day, and he soon began to live with Mary Rynar Moore, whom he hired from her owner at $48 per year. They had one child, which in accordance with the law followed the mother in slavery.

Thomas continued to save his money, and he was finally able to buy Rynar's freedom for $350. Their three additional children were thus born free, since the status of the children followed that of the mother. However, when the General Assembly failed to pass a bill that would have made her emancipation official, Thomas slipped his wife and the free children aboard a boat heading for New York. They went to Brooklyn and were taken in by Robert H. Cousins.

Determined to join his family, Thomas Jones in September 1849 bargained with the steward aboard the brig *Bell* and for $8 was allowed to stow away. By the time the ship anchored off New York, the captain had discovered the runaway slave and was threatening to turn the fugitive over to the authorities.

While the captain was ashore, Thomas lashed several empty barrels together as a raft and jumped ship. He reached the shore and was befriended.

Reunited with his wife and children in Brooklyn, Thomas Jones took up preaching as a means of livelihood. He later moved to Boston and in 1849 dictated his story, which was published by an abolitionist group.

Camden County Slave Bought His Freedom

THREE TIMES MOSES GRANDY SAVED enough money to buy his freedom. Twice his master took the money and kept him in bondage.

By his mid-fifties, however, through the help of white friends, he had bought not only his own freedom but also that of his wife, son and grandchild. He then made his way to England and published a little book that was widely distributed by the abolitionists.

Moses Grandy was born about 1786 on the farm of William Grandy in Camden County, North Carolina. His master was a "hard drinking man," but Moses was treated well because he was the favorite playmate of James, the master's son.

When William Grandy died, however, Moses was given to James who was, of course, not of legal age. Consequently Moses was hired out to the highest bidder each year, the money going to the account of his former playmate.

He had a succession of temporary masters, the first being Enoch Sawyer, one of the county's most prominent citizens and the local ferry keeper. Moses charged later than Sawyer was a hard master, forcing him to work in the winter without shoes. He sometimes aroused hogs in order to warm his feet on the ground upon which they had slept.

Some of his temporary masters, like Richard Furley (Furlow?), were good to him. While with Furley, Moses was a carboy, driving lumber from the Dismal Swamp. In fact, Moses was allowed to hire himself out for piecework, and he made more than enough to pay Furley for his annual bid. Consequently, the young slave began saving money.

But then James Grandy came of age, and, forgetting their childhood friendship, he required Moses to pay even more for the privilege of working for wages. The young slave ran boats through the Dismal Swamp Canal and added to his savings.

He married a woman belonging to Enoch Sawyer, but about eight months afterward, his wife was sold and taken away. He never saw her again.

Nevertheless, the industrious Moses finally saved enough money to buy himself from James Grandy. His master, however, took his $600 and refused to go to the courthouse and sign the emancipation papers. Instead, Grandy sold Moses to a Mr. Trewitt who again put him to work on canal boats.

Once again Moses, after several years, had saved enough money to buy himself. Only after he had paid Trewitt did the slave discover that his master had defaulted and that, as chattel property, he was to be sold again to satisfy the creditors.

This time he was purchased by Enoch Sawyer who allowed him to continue as boat captain in return for a portion of his wages. Moses remarried and saved money, though not enough.

Finally, Moses persuaded Captain Edward Miner of Deep Creek to buy him with the understanding that he would eventually purchase his own freedom. After several years, Moses for the third time paid $600 for his emancipation. This time the honest master let him go.

Moses Grandy continued working aboard coastal vessels, then began taking longer trips—to New England and to the Indies. He saved enough to purchase the freedom of his wife, a son and grandson. Six other children remained in slavery at New Orleans. It was to enable him to earn enough to purchase their freedom and that of a sister that he decided to go to England and allow his story to be published in book form.

The little book described one of the cruelties practiced by some slaveholders. Moses's mother, old and blind, was given a miserable hut in the woods. There she lived alone, scratching out a little corn from a small plot of cleared land. Occasionally fellow slaves shared their skimpy rations or caught a fish for her. Moses Grandy wrote: "No care is taken of them, except, perhaps, that a little ground is cleared about the hut, on which the old slave, if able, may raise a little corn. As far as the owner is concerned, they live or die as it happens; it is just the same as turning out an old horse."

Let's Honor James Boone
This Time

I<small>N</small> S<small>COTT</small> C<small>OUNTY IN SOUTHWESTERN</small> Virginia stands a state highway historical marker reading, "Near here, October 10, 1773, James Boone, son of Daniel Boone, and Henry Russell, members of Boone's party on the way to Kentucky, were surprised and killed by Indians."

That is probably the only monument to James Boone, for there are no towns, counties, highways, wines or television shows named for him. Such names are traced back to his father, skipping over James as if he never existed.

North Carolinians, however, ought to take some pride in James. After all, unlike his father, he was a native of our state and grew up along the tributaries of the Yadkin River in the area in and around the present Davie County.

James, the first child of Daniel and Rebecca Bryan Boone, was born in 1757, only a few years after Daniel had come with his parents from Pennsylvania to the backwoods of North Carolina.

Virtually nothing is known of James's childhood, but it is not difficult to picture the very special place that he occupied in Daniel Boone's affection. Although Rebecca gave birth to eight other children, undoubtedly the first-born son received favored attention from his father. Daniel, who spent much of his time—particularly in fall and winter—in scouting and hunting, often took the lad along, teaching him the skills of a frontiersman.

Although Daniel Boone had explored the area several times before, it was not until 1773 that he sold his North Carolina property and packed his remaining worldly goods upon horses. In September he, his family and a number of friends began the long trek to their new homes in what is now Kentucky.

In the Clinch River valley of southwestern Virginia they received aid from William Russell, a pioneer settler there, and then pushed on. After doing some mental figuring, however, Daniel decided that they needed more foodstuffs and tools, so he asked James to take a party back to Russell's and pick up the additional supplies.

The impetuous teenager rode off alone. He arrived safely, but Russell insisted that his own son, Henry, and several of his hands return to camp with James. After all, the Shawnees were in an ugly mood over the white incursions. On the way back to the Boone camp, the group became lost, and as night fell, they decided to camp near Walden's Creek.

During the night a party of Shawnees saw the light from the campfire, slipped up and fired into the sleeping men. Several were killed, James and Henry were wounded in the hip, and one of Russell's slaves slipped into the underbrush and witnessed the agonizing hours that followed.

Instead of ending the misery of the two wounded boys, the Shawnees proceeded to torture them with knives. The atrocity was all the more incomprehensible because the leader of the band was Big Jim, a Shawnee who had often visited the Boone cabin and whom Daniel had counted as a friend. The pleas of the youths that their pain be ended with one blow of a tomahawk were ignored, and the slicing of strips of flesh continued until they both finally died. James was only sixteen years old, and unknown to the party, they had reached within three miles of his father's camp. Three miles between death and safety.

The bodies were found the next morning, and James was buried nearby. Daniel, upon hearing the news, prepared for an anticipated attack upon his camp. But he also took time out to visit the fresh grave of his son, making sure that it was covered with logs to prevent violation of the body by animals.

While Daniel wanted to push on to Kentucky, the incident caused the remaining families to lose heart, and they turned back. Daniel and Rebecca and their family, however, occupied a vacant cabin and remained in the Clinch River area until 1775 when they finally reached their destination. Another son, Israel, also lost his life in an Indian raid in 1782. Daniel and Rebecca later moved to Missouri, where he died in 1820.

Woman Admitted to State Bar in 1878 After Debate

THE EDITOR OF THE GREENSBORO *North State* sighed and asked, "What next?"
What next, indeed. The Civil War had been over only a few years, and already North Carolina was yielding to the social revolution creeping down from the North. Six years before, the Medical Society had admitted a woman to honorary membership, and now, in 1878, a "modest, timid, unassuming young lady" had won admission to the bar.

The "sprightly brunette, of medium size, an intellectual cast of countenance, though not strikingly handsome," was Tabitha Ann Holton, the twenty-three-year-old daughter of a Methodist Protestant minister in Guilford County.

Dressed "neatly but not gorgeously," Tabitha appeared with her brother, Samuel Melanchton Holton, and eighteen other male applicants before the staid old state Supreme Court in January 1878. The justices lost little time in calling for a recess to figure out how to handle such a surprising development.

After recovering their courage and making a fast reference to certain statues, the court reconvened and invited Miss Holton and her attorney, Judge Albion W. Tourgee, to present her request.

That request was simple: Tabitha wanted to take the bar examination. She hastened to explain, however, that she did not intend to practice in North Carolina; rather, she wanted to go to Kansas, where several women had practiced successfully. The latter state, however, had a two-year residency requirement, so she wanted a North Carolina license, which would be recognized immediately in Kansas.

But, the judges observed, the statues governing admission to the bar clearly used the male gender. Besides, said William H. Battle, who opposed her admission, no Southern lady should be "permitted to sully her sweetness by breathing the pestiferous air of the court room."

To the former observation Judge Tourgee argued that the mere technicality of language should not be allowed to hold back social evolution, and pointed to court decisions which had extended the meaning of the pre-war term "free white" to black men after emancipation.

In response to Battle's concern, Tourgee suggested that allowing women freedom of choice in the professions would increase their means of self-support and prevent them from falling into poverty, immorality and vice. In other words, better a female attorney than a streetwalker.

The five justices were impressed by both Tourgee's arguments and the modesty and charm of Miss Holton. Even more persuasive, however, was her keen knowledge of the law. They noted that she was rather timid in conversation but displayed "fine colloquial powers when brought out."

Tabitha was permitted to take the examination, and she passed with ease. Two months later when Judge McKay administered the oath to her, North Carolina became the sixth state in the union (and the first in the South) to license a woman lawyer.

Miss Holton won her license without ever having attended law school. In fact, she had no particular preceptor in her studies, though various members of the Greensboro bar had lent her books and examined her from time to time.

Even after her admission to the bar, many men were reluctant to accept the precedent. The editor of the *North State* summarized the situation this way: "Some of the older members of the profession . . . feel very badly to think a woman has become a member of the North Carolina bar; but if woman is lowered by such association, whose fault is it, her own or that of her comrades?"

Quaint Notebook Describes North Carolina Deaths

T HE TYPESETTER SHOULD GET A medal if he (or she) can set the following entry correctly: "Wm Davis age 100.8 dide oc 5 1841. ware old Solder in rev wre and got his thie brok in laste fite at king monte . he wars farmer and made brandy and never had Drunker in famly."

Only punctuation has been added in this first entry in the book of deaths kept by Jacob Carpenter from 1841 to 1915. Today the same obituary might simply read: "Died Oct. 5, 1841: William Davis, age 108, Revolutionary War soldier who broke his thigh at the battle of King's Mountain; farmer and sober distiller." Somehow, though, the flavor gets lost in the modern translation.

"Uncle Jake" Carpenter lived in Three Mile Creek near Crossnore in Avery County. His house was two miles up the gap from the main road, and he was familiar with all the families in that region of the mountains. Each time someone died, he wrote down the facts, adding his personal comments—sometimes favorable to the deceased, sometimes not. Later he recopied the entries into a daybook. He died in 1920 at the age of eighty-seven.

Some years ago Denise M. Abbey, with the aid of Mary M. Sloop and Theron Dellinger, prepared a typed copy of the "anthology of death," and recently Dr. Chalmers G. Davidson of Davidson College contributed it to the North Carolina Collection at Chapel Hill. The quaint item is valuable as the only register of deaths in Avery County for the nineteenth century.

Nearly every record evokes a smile from the reader. The wife of Franky Davis, for instance, died in 1842, and Uncle Jake noted that she had had the "nirv" to fight wolves all night to save her calf. According to him, she "throde fier chonks to save caff'" at a campsite.

Six years later Ben Blalock, age forty, was "cild June 5 by tree cot far conny." Translated, that meant that Ben ran the wrong way when he chopped down a tree to get at a coon.

Old Charley Kiney, who died in 1852 at age seventy-two, must have been quite a fellow. Uncle Jake wrote that Charley had four "wimin" and forty-two children, all of whom went to preaching together and got along "smoth." To feed them, Charley made brandy and killed from seventy-five to eighty hogs a year.

Of his own father by the same name, Carpenter wrote proudly that he was a farmer and cooper who made hogsheads and brandy. He lived to be eighty-six, raised twelve children, and never had to see a doctor.

In 1859 Mary Diling was killed in a mill when her dress was caught around the shaft. Carpenter had to help pull her body out. Nine years later Peggy Wise, "granny womin," died.

Young Joseph Carpenter was killed in 1862. What more poetic tribute could there be to the young soldier than this: "hey fot for his contery los his lif ."

Soonsy Ollis, who died in 1871, must have been the greatest hunter in the area. He was said to have killed deer, turkeys and rattlesnakes by the hundreds. Henry Barrier apparently was the champion bear hunter, though.

Abraham Johnson died in 1881 at the age of about one hundred seven. A farmer and operator of an iron forge, he was said to have loved liquor but "never wars drunk in his days." Steven Buckanon was described as a "precher babus"—that is, a Baptist preacher. Samuel Hoskins was called a "grate lier."

Perhaps the most touching entry in the little book of deaths is that concerning Margaret Carpenter, who died at eighty-seven in 1875. According to Uncle Jake, Margaret was so poor as a child that she had no bed on which to sleep, having instead to use a deerskin until she got married. No woman, he proudly noted, had to sleep on deerskins after she got married.

Jacob Carpenter apparently wrote in his little book for his own information. He probably never imagined that in doing so he was making a contribution to history.

Cross Woodis Oldest North Carolinian?

WHO WAS THE OLDEST PERSON ever to live in North Carolina? We may never know, but one candidate for the distinction was Cross Woodis who complained before his death about 1880 that liquor had shortened his years.

He had done pretty well, though, for according to his biographer, Woodis was one hundred thirty years old when he died. If we base his age on the census of 1860 when he was listed as one hundred, he would have been only one hundred twenty at the time of his death. But what difference would ten years make at that age?

Sometime after he was a century old, Cross Woodis gave up hard drink, but he still enjoyed chewing tobacco, smoking his pipe and playing his fiddle. Most of all, he enjoyed telling tall tales.

We would perhaps know nothing of Cross Woodis except for a tiny sketch published in 1905 by Alfred Nixon, a former teacher, county surveyor, sheriff and school superintendent, who served as Lincoln County's clerk of superior court until his death in 1924. Nixon, who as a youngster knew Woodis well, based his information on the old man's own account.

A mulatto born free but bound to a white man named Curtis until he was twenty-one, Cross Woodis, according to the census records, was born in Mecklenburg County long before the Revolution. He spent many years in Cabarrus County but lived in Lincoln County in his advanced years. He had a cabin on the farm of William King near Catawba Springs.

As a young man, Woodis married a free black woman who, when the Southern states began restricting the rights of free Negroes, insisted that the couple move to the free state of Ohio. Woodis told her to go ahead with her relatives and he would follow. He never did, except for a visit. After years of separation from his first wife, he married another free black woman in North Carolina.

Apparently Cross Woodis was primarily a farmer, but he worked at various jobs—fisherman, hunter, horse racer, well digger and water witch. With a forked peach tree sprout, he was almost unerring in locating water for his clients. The census taker of 1860 reported that Woodis was the only farmer in Lincoln County growing rice—perhaps a natural outgrowth of his ability to produce water from the ground.

Woodis was remembered as shriveled and stooped but retaining a remarkable degree of his senses, particularly his memory and wit. He claimed to have killed a British soldier while guarding a cache of guns during the Revolution, a claim that Nixon accepted as true. In later years neighbors sought out "Uncle Cross" to hear his stories, many of which he exaggerated.

In Cabarrus County, Woodis said, he dug a well so deep that when he hit water he could hear roosters crowing in China. Always on the lookout for bee colonies, he said he once found a tree filled with honey along the Catawba River, but that when he tried to get to the honey the tree toppled into the water, sweetening the river "five miles up, and I don't know how fur down, sir."

Nixon once asked Woodis what was the biggest lie he ever told. Indignantly, the old man replied, "By de gods, sir, Mr. Nixon, I never told a lie in my life." Then, with a slowly developing grin, he admitted that he had just told his biggest lie.

Throughout the area the ultimate characterization of a prevaricator was to be accused of being "as big a liar as Old Cross." But it was all in fun. The centenarian was loved by both whites and blacks, and Nixon wrote, "I never heard anything dishonorable charged to his account."

Cross Woodis died at the home of a daughter in Mecklenburg County about 1880 and was buried at a Presbyterian church for blacks at Caldwell, a few miles from Cowan's Ford.

Battle Against
"Germ of Laziness"

Sixty-five years ago a strange battle was beginning in North Carolina. The campaign involved Northern money, a small band of dedicated doctors and thousands of North Carolinians unknowingly infected by a debilitating parasite.

Although Southerners generally rejected as libelous the accusation that they were lazy, many scientists were convinced that diseases associated with the soil, climate and sanitary conditions were indeed sapping the strength of the population. It was not until 1902, however, that Dr. Charles H. Stiles received widespread attention for his findings about a chief culprit.

Dr. Stiles, a doctor in the United States Public Health Service who spent part of his time at the Marine Hospital at Wilmington, concluded that a formidable enemy was the hookworm—a small worm which attached itself to the lining of the human intestine and sucked the blood of its victim.

One person might be infected with hundreds or even thousands of these parasites, which contributed to anemia, stunted growth and lethargy. Weakened by hookworms, the victim was easy prey for other diseases such as tuberculosis.

The doctor found that the incidence of hookworm was heaviest in the Southern states, particularly in areas with warm loamy soil. The eggs of the worm were passed through feces and, upon hatching, reentered human bodies most often through bare feet. This stage of infection led to a rash called ground itch or dew poisoning, but the real damage began when the parasite found its way to the intestine.

The publicity associated with Dr. Stiles's findings and proposed remedies angered many Southerners. In North Carolina, Governor Robert B. Glenn, Captain S.A.

Ashe, and others saw the anti-hookworm proposals as another Yankee insult to the South. Southerners were just as healthy and energetic as people from the North, they claimed.

One Tar Heel, though, enthusiastically supported Dr. Stiles. After a meeting on a train headed for New York, Walter Hines Page escorted the doctor to the offices of John D. Rockefeller. The wealthy industrialist was impressed, and he gave a million dollars for the establishment of the Rockefeller Sanitary Commission, which began a five-year campaign against hookworm in the South.

In North Carolina the sanitary commission, a branch of the state board of health, was headed by Dr. John A. Ferrell. During the first three years a small staff conducted an educational campaign in the central and eastern part of the state, but by 1913 the commission adopted the "dispensary" method of conducting county campaigns in which a doctor and a microscopist held clinics in various communities, examining specimens and treating infected persons on the spot.

Most counties welcomed the campaign, particularly since treatment was free to the citizens, and the county commissioners had to put up only a few hundred dollars. Occasional hostility was overcome only through diplomacy and demonstrated results. Eventually just one county—Ashe —failed to cooperate, and few citizens remained unconvinced of the merits of the battle when dramatic results were produced.

The treatment was no fun. Without food for twelve hours, the victim was given a dose of Epsom salts, followed by capsules of powdered thymol mixed with milk sugar, followed by more salts.

But the battle within the body was only the beginning; an even more difficult task was the promotion of improved sanitation, including the proper design of outdoor privies, the source of much of the contagion.

A survey prior to the beginning of treatment indicated that 70 percent of those examined in Wayne County had hookworm, as did more than half of those examined in Beaufort, Cumberland, Duplin, New Hanover, Pender, Pitt and Sampson. Generally the percentage of infected whites was more than double that of blacks.

While the battle against hookworm was never completely won, the work of the sanitary commission brought astonishing results by awakening citizens to the relationship between unsanitary conditions and the prevalence of diseases. Resident doctors began paying more attention to parasitic diseases, more people began wearing shoes and "worming" became a routine in many families.

A survey in 1936 showed a 700 percent decline in hookworm infection in Pitt County, with marked though less drastic improvements in other counties.

Even so, the hookworm still has not been eradicated, particularly among farm children without sanitary toilets. The "germ of laziness," however, has been on the defensive ever since Drs. Stiles and Ferrell, with Rockefeller money, declared war on it in 1910.

Peter Francisco—Hercules of the Revolution

Peter Francisco was a Virginian, but his exploits at the Battle of Guilford Courthouse in 1781 won him fame in North Carolina. A few years ago the postal service issued a commemorative stamp in honor of the man who exhibited "super human" strength.

Nothing is known of the European origin of the young lad who at about age five was left behind at City Point, Virginia, when a ship sailed way in 1765.

The silver buckles of his shoes were engraved "P.F.," and his swarthy complexion suggested a possible Iberian birth. Unable to speak English, the boy was placed in the poorhouse but was later befriended by Judge Anthony Winston who made Peter a part of his own family at Hunting Towers, his home in Buckingham County.

Here Peter learned English, worked on the farm and grew and grew and grew. In fact, he was twice the size of most boys, and perhaps this explains why he was not sent away to school.

In 1775 young Peter accompanied the judge to Richmond where they heard Patrick Henry make his immortal "Liberty or Death" speech.

The boy was so excited that he wanted to enlist immediately in the Whig forces, but he was persuaded to wait until the next year when he joined the 10th Virginia Regiment of Continental troops. Still only sixteen years old, Peter stood nearly six-and-a-half feet tall and weighed two hundred sixty pounds.

Following the Battle of Brandywine in which, despite being wounded, Peter astounded both the Americans and the British with his physical strength, General Washington was said to have ordered a five-foot sword made specifically for him.

In battle the oversized youngster received sword or bayonet wounds but continued fighting; at Powell's Hook, for instance, a wound in the thigh failed to prevent him from rushing into the British lines and killing two soldiers.

In the Battle of Camden, Peter moved a one thousand, one hundred-pound canon without assistance, then plucked a British soldier from his horse and presented the animal to Colonel William Mayo, whose life he had just saved.

At Guilford Courthouse Francisco was recorded as having killed eleven Englishman with his "terrible broad sword" after his thigh was slit open. It is not known how many he killed before being wounded. He was then left on the field for dead, but soon he was on the move again. Today a large granite shaft commemorates his heroism at Guilford.

One of the most famous engravings of the Revolution pictured Francisco single-handedly routing nine British soldiers who attempted to capture him in Amelia County, Virginia, in 1781.

Another engraving showed him tossing a giant across a fence. According to the stories surrounding the latter, a Kentuckian by the name of Pamphlett, who styled himself the strongest man in the country, came to challenge Francisco.

To show his own strength, Pamphlett twice lifted Peter from the ground. Then Francisco picked his visitor up twice, then again, this time tossing him across a fence. The surprised Kentuckian suggested that Peter might be so kind as to hand him his horse, and—according to this story—that request was promptly obeyed.

After the war Peter decided he needed an education. He entered a country school, whose schoolmaster later wrote "Francisco would take me in his right hand and pass me over the room, playing my head against the ceiling as though I had been a doll." The schoolmaster weighed one hundred ninety pounds.

Peter entered business and married three times. In 1825 he moved to Richmond and served six years as sergeant-at-arms in the Virginia House of Delegates. When he died in 1831, Virginia officials gathered for his burial with full military honors.

Stories of Peter Francisco's strength may have been exaggerated over the years, but there is ample evidence that he was physically one of the most powerful men ever to serve in American forces.

Remarks on his brute strength and strong character were left by many of the prominent leaders of the Revolution, including General Lafayette with whom he enjoyed a warm friendship. Peter Francisco was truly the "Hercules of the Revolution."

Tar Heel Governor Was Jinxed

H E BECAME ONE OF NORTH Carolina's largest landowners, yet he died virtually a pauper. He generously offered himself as surety for trusted friends, yet their defaults led to the dissipation of his fortune. He gave the University of North Carolina its first large gift, yet the university's attorney had him jailed for debt.

In his two terms as governor he advocated humanitarian reforms, yet upon his death his friends had to secretly bury his body to keep creditors from claiming it. He was honored by having a town named after him, but the residents later changed the name to Southport. The university named a building for him, but it is better known today as Playmakers Theatre.

He fought at least three duels, a bullet from one of which identified his deteriorated body when, after many years, it was finally given a decent burial in a churchyard.

Such was the fate of Benjamin Smith, governor of North Carolina from 1810 to 1811.

Though the subject was born in 1756 in Charleston, South Carolina, he was the grandson of "King" Roger Moore of Orton Plantation, and upon his marriage to Sarah Dry, daughter of the prominent William Dry of Brunswick, Benjamin settled on the lower Cape Fear. Donald R. Lennon of East Carolina University, his biographer, concludes that by the time Smith was thirty-four years old he was the wealthiest planter in Brunswick County with two hundred twenty-one slaves, and that by 1800 he held more than sixty thousand acres of land.

Such wealth dictated public service, and Smith served in the general assembly almost continuously from 1783 to 1810, including five years as speaker of the senate. In 1784 he was elected to the Confederation Congress, but he chose not to take his seat. He represented his county in both state conventions called to consider ratification of the federal constitution. For thirty-five years he was a member of the board of trustees of the University of North Carolina, and for three years he was grand master of North Carolina Masons. In 1794 he was commissioned a brigadier general in the state militia, a rank that apparently gave rise to an inflated account of his Revolutionary War service.

Long before Smith became governor, however, a series of complicated and unsuccessful financial ventures, including his role as surety for trusted friends, began to undermine the fortune of the master of Belvidere Plantation. For instance, James Read was charged with skullduggery while collector of the port of Wilmington, and the federal government brought suit to recover its losses. Smith, Read's surety, was forced to give up much of his property, including Smith Island, named for his ancestor, Landgrave Thomas Smith.

To the University of North Carolina Smith gave the twenty thousand acres of Tennessee land awarded him for his service in the Revolution. But in 1812, the university brought suit against Carleton Walker, for whom Smith was a surety, and the former governor was jailed for a short time. The land, incidentally, was ill fated. It was ceded to the Chickasaw Indians but in 1810 an earthquake hit the area, dropping the surface and forming Reelfoot Lake.

Franklin Square in Smithville was a gift from Smith, but in 1889 the town's name was changed to Southport. University of North Carolina's Smith Hall, constructed in the 1850s, was named for him, but it too is now better known by another designation—Playmakers Theatre.

It was in 1805 that Benjamin Smith uttered disparaging remarks about his kinsmen, the Moores, and he was promptly challenged to a duel by Maurice Moore. Astride the line between the two Carolinas, Smith was wounded in the side by one of Moore's bullets.

Tradition notwithstanding, the former governor appears not to have died in prison but rather in his home in Smithville on January 27, 1826. Nor did his creditors take possession of his body, though they undoubtedly would have except for the prompt and secretive action of his friends who spirited the body away and buried it a few miles from town. Several decades later, when public opinion concerning imprisonment for debt had changed, one of the friends led a party to the site, exhumed the remains and re-interred him in the churchyard at St. Philips Church in Brunswick Town.

Not until a hundred years after his death was a proper marker finally provided for a man who had been one of North Carolina's leading citizens and who had served the state as its chief executive for two years.

Babe Ruth Hit First Home Run in North Carolina

NORTH CAROLINIANS WATCHING ON APRIL 8, 1974, as Hank Aaron hit his seven hundred fifteenth home run were probably as pleased as citizens of other states, but perhaps they should have felt a twinge of regret. After all, Babe Ruth hit his first home run as a professional player in Fayetteville. Tar Heels, therefore, felt a particular kinship to the "Sultan of Swat," whose record Aaron broke.

That first homer was hit in March, 1914, and it came in a Baltimore Orioles intrasquad game between the "Sparrows" and the "Buzzards." Ruth played shortstop for the Buzzards for half the game and then finished in the box. Late in the game he hit a three hundred fifty-footer over the right field fence.

That was a pretty impressive accomplishment for the nineteen-year-old youngster whom owner Jack Dunn of the Orioles had signed out of a reform school in Baltimore for a hundred dollars a month. Ruth himself later said that Dunn "signed the papers which made him accountable to a Maryland court for my welfare and . . . he came to the barred gate of St. Mary's to claim me." Within a few days the club with its new recruit was in Fayetteville for spring training, enticed there by Hyman Fleishman and Jim Johnson who paid for the team's room and board.

Fayetteville made a lasting impression on Ruth. He later said, "I got to some bigger places than Fayetteville after that, but darn few as exciting." In fact, it was there that he acquired the nickname "Babe." He recalled that in his first appearance in the field Dunn "practically led me by the hand from the dressing room to the pitcher's box," and as they went an older player yelled, "Look at Dunnie and his new babe."

He added that another incident helped establish the nickname. He delighted in playing around with the elevator in the Lafayette Hotel, and once when he drew his head out of the shaft just before the elevator came down, a player commented, "You're just a babe in the woods." After that, George Herman Ruth was simply Babe Ruth or, as he became famous, the "Bambino."

About his first home run, Ruth said, "I hit it as I hit all the others, by taking a good gander at the pitch as it came up to the plate, twisting my body into a back swing and then hitting it as hard as I could swing. I don't have to tell you what it did to me, inside, but the effect on Dunnie and the others was easy to see, too." The club's owner knew he had a star in the making.

We have two eyewitness reports of that historic game. Roger H. Pippen, a teammate and reporter for the *Baltimore American*, wrote in 1950 that he measured the three hundred fifty-foot distance of the homer after the game. He added, "today, with the lively ball that wouldn't be considered a long clout. In those days, with the dead apple, it was so unusual the people in Baltimore thought I was having a drunken dream when I flashed the news back home." Pippen recalled that in an exhibition game in Wilmington the same spring, Ruth struck out the then famous home-run hitter, Frank Baker, to defeat the powerful Athletics.

Maurice Flieshman, a Fayetteville businessman, last year recounted his presence as a batboy for the team. It was largely through Flieshman's persistence that in 1952 the Department of Archives and History erected on highway US 301, a highway historical marker commemorating the event. Appropriately, in connection with the unveiling, the Baltimore Orioles played the Philadelphia Athletics in an exhibition game.

Hamp Rich—Carolina's Champion Monument Builder

IF SAMUEL JOHNSON HAD HIS James Boswell, Daniel Boone had his Hamp Rich. Nobody ever had a more dedicated alter ego. His full name was Joseph Hampton Rich, and between 1913 and 1940 he was responsible for the placement of hundreds of Daniel Boone tablets from Virginia Beach to San Francisco and from Florida to Michigan and Massachusetts. And when he thought the old Indian fighter had been sufficiently honored, he began building monuments to other pioneers and to the Indians.

Hamp Rich's interest in Daniel Boone came naturally, for he grew up only a few miles from the graves of Boone's parents in Davie County. He was born July 14, 1874, the son of Samuel Chase and Betty Caroline McMahan Rich.

He graduated from Wake Forest College in 1898 and then attended the Southern Baptist Seminary in Louisville. After preaching and teaching a while, he bought a printing press and operated the Piedmont Printing Company in Winston-Salem and published a newspaper called *The Labor Leader*.

In 1913, he founded the Boone Trail Highway and Memorial Association with the purpose of building "an arterial highway to reclaim the counties of the northwestern part of the state in honor of Daniel Boone."

Soon Rich engaged a sculptor named Henley to design the Daniel Boone tablet, and he began his remarkable career of peddling them all over the country. The Navy gave him four hundred pounds of metal from the U.S.S. *Maine*, which had been scuttled in 1912, and a little bit of this metal was mixed into each tablet. Nobody ever figured out the connection between Boone and the battleship.

The trail to Kentucky having been marked, Rich began working on a transcontinental Boone Trail from Virginia Beach to San Francisco. He made a cross-country trip in 1925 and claimed to have spoken to fifty thousand school children.

When questioned about the marker constructed at the Golden Gate, Rich explained that though Boone never got that far, he dreamed a lot about the Pacific.

The indefatigable Rich conceived a "Coal-to-Cotton Highway" from West Virginia through the Carolinas and a "Detroit to St. Augustine Cross-Line," along both of which he built Boone markers. Then he went to Boston, spoke at twenty schools, and put up two markers there.

In the 1930s, Rich concluded that maybe Daniel Boone had enough markers in his honor, so he began working on an "Appalachian Indian Road and Buffalo Trail," along which he placed tablets honoring the buffalo and the Indian chief, Sequoyah. He also put up tablets to David Crockett, Thomas Burke and Nathaniel Brock.

His travels and experiences were described in the association's little paper, *Boone Trail Herald*, which Rich published sporadically in Winston-Salem from 1924 to 1938. By the outbreak of World War II, he could claim to have placed three hundred fifty-eight tablets from the Atlantic to the Pacific and from the Great Lakes to Florida.

His arrowheads and tablets may still be seen around North Carolina, sometimes overrun by vines, sometimes defaced by vandals, often at places never heard of by Boone. They honor not only the pioneer spirit but also that of Hamp Rich, North Carolina's champion monument builder.

Largest Mail-Order Liquor Business

THE LIQUID WAS DESCRIBED AS being used daily "by frail children, invalid ladies and diseased, suffering men for the betterment of their health." In fact, it was called "the best medicine in the world!"

"It" was Casper's Whiskey, made by "Honest North Carolina People."

John L. Casper published a thirty-two-page booklet to extol the merits of his products and to explain, "I claim to be an honest man and I sell honest whiskies. I guess I am the only real, living man engaged in the mail-order whiskey business who is not afraid to show his face." And there, on page one, mustachioed John Casper's photograph was signed "yours for honest whiskies."

That was back in 1904, and Casper took great pains to explain that whiskey making was a time-honored occupation in the Blue Ridge Mountains.

Proudly he recounted that his family had for generations been "engaged in the manufacture of this product after their secret formula," mainly for their own use. Then in 1861 his grandfather began selling the products of his distillery.

When J.G. Casper returned from four years in the army during the Civil War, he joined his father as an apprentice, eventually took over the business, and expanded it. This may have been Private James C. Casper from Rowan County who served in Company K, 4th North Carolina Regiment.

Finally, before the end of the century, J.C.'s son, John L. Casper, became actively connected with the still and took over its operation. Soon John acquired more stills, and by 1904 he owned an even dozen in western North Carolina.

But he did not stop there. In the face of competition from "greedy unprincipled dealers," he convinced the owners of twenty-one other distillers that there was a need for controlled quality and mail-order sales.

He formed the Casper Company and contracted for these twenty-one other distilleries to add their entire output to that of his own dozen stills. In Winston-Salem he constructed a six-story fire-proof building covering a city block.

The stock from the various stills was brought to the receiving room in seasoned oak barrels whose interiors had been charred over maple wood fires. After being tested initially to determine acceptable quality, the liquid was aged in rooms with glass roofs so that the sun's rays could strike the barrels at right angles. This provided an average temperature of about one hundred twenty degrees in summer and ninety degrees in winter.

The heat slowly forced evaporation of impurities through the charred barrels, leaving the pure whiskey in a mild, mellow form. After aging—sometimes for many years—the whiskey was filtered through huge tanks packed with layers of white sand, maple charcoal, linen and heavy woolens.

The filtered whiskey was then placed in two hundred twenty-five-gallon barrels and tested. If Internal Revenue Service officials approved its quality, tax stamps were affixed.

As sales required, the liquid was poured into bottles, jugs, kegs, and demijohns ranging from small flasks to five-gallon vessels. By 1904 the Casper Company handled up to two thousand orders per day. In November and December, the plant operated twenty-four hours a day. It claimed a quarter of a million customers around the world.

Prices ranged from $1.50 per gallon for three-year-old "Mountain" whiskey to $3.80 per gallon for "Gold Band," claimed to be "without a vestige of headache." A hundred half-pints of corn whiskey could be bought for $15.00. Peach brandy sold for $2.50 and scuppernong wine for 85¢ per gallon For $1.25 one could get a quart of "Very Old Private Stock" in a glass bottle in the form of a naked lady.

Casper's success was advertised in large letters running the length of his block-long plant in Winston-Salem: "Largest building in the United States devoted exclusively to the mail-order whiskey business."

But the days of the business where numbered, for four years later North Carolinians voted for statewide prohibition. Casper later entered the grocery business and operated a "Basketeria." He died July 22, 1921, and was buried in Salem Cemetery.

Spanish Invade North Carolina

SPANISH CONTROL IN NORTH CAROLINA? Hardly, but there were times in the 1740s when the Spanish did indeed get temporary footholds in the colony.

Throughout the curiously named War of Jenkin's Ear and King George's War, Spanish privateers operated along the coast, darting back to safety in Florida when necessary. They were a threat to the defenseless residents of the Outer Banks, and as early as 1741 they established a shore station on Ocracoke Island. Smaller vessels sailed into the shallow sounds, capturing and intimidating Colonial vessels.

By 1747, in the words of Governor Gabriel Johnston, the Spanish boldly "landed at Ocracock (sic), Core sound, Bear Inlet, and Cape Fear, where they killed several of his Majesty's subjects, burned some ships and several small Vessels, carried off some Negroes, and slaughtered a Vast number of Black Cattle and Hogs . . ." During that same summer the Spanish captured the town of Beaufort and held it for three days. The danger of Spanish occupation of North Carolina began to appear real to residents of the seaboard.

The climax to these threats came the following year when, at dawn on September 4, 1748, citizens of the town of Brunswick on the Cape Fear River awoke to the sound of guns from two Spanish ships and an American ship that the Spaniards had captured. Simultaneously, armed Spaniards, who had landed downstream, invaded the town. In panic the residents fled, leaving the foreigners in possession of Brunswick.

While the invaders plundered the homes and shops, carrying their booty to waiting ships, Captain William Dry sought to organize the militiamen. However, in their flight from the Spanish, many of them had left their firearms behind.

Still, a few armed men sneaked back into town and surprised the plunderers who, assuming the American force to be larger than it was, sought to retreat to one of the ships. Nearly a dozen of them were killed and about thirty were taken prisoner.

The Spaniards who reached the ship opened fire on the town, but suddenly and inexplicably, the *Fortuna* blew up, killing most of the men aboard. Only a few escaped to become prisoners, and most of them were wounded.

The remaining Spaniards aboard the captured American ship began shelling Brunswick and might have obliterated the town had they not realized that their own men, now prisoners of the Americans, might also be killed. So they sailed off, taking with them that portion of the plunder that had not gone down with the sunken ship, but leaving behind about a hundred dead comrades and thirty or so prisoners.

Strangely, little documentation remains of the "Spanish Alarm," as the period of Spanish depredations is called in history. There is no good contemporary narrative account of substance, and much of what we know comes from claims for compensation. Joseph Blake, for instance, itemized his claim for "Sundry Ferryages of Men & Horses over & back again by Ferry, on accompt of the Spaniardses landing and plundering Brunswick, and ferrying sundry Messengers backwards & forwards. . . ."

William Dry's claim for nearly £700 sterling listed such items as pork, beef, rice, rum, powder, balls, burying of dead Spaniards and "for assisting to gett the Guns & anchors, & c., on shoar out of the wreck." Claims of the firm of Davies and Mackenzie listed flints, guns, cutlasses, cartouch boxes, lanthorn, salt, paper and fourteen gallons of rum and wine. Dr. Samuel Green charged £143 for taking care of wounded Spaniards, two of them for twenty-four days.

The Spaniards were never again a serious threat to North Carolina after these aggravating experiences, and they left behind no lasting scars. If tradition can be believed, however, a rare souvenir of their attack on Brunswick now hangs in St. James Church in Wilmington—a painting, *Ecce Homo*, said to have been salvaged from a wrecked privateer.

John Lawson's Journey

IN 1700 JOHN LAWSON LEFT Charleston, South Carolina, on the first extensively recorded exploration of the backcountry of the two Carolinas. His account remains a valuable source of information on the land and the first Americans—the Indians.

Little is known of Lawson's background in Great Britain, though he was obviously a man of education and some means. His interest in botany may have led him to the land that had been settled by Europeans for less than a century. At Charleston the Lords Proprietors commissioned Lawson to explore the inland section of their colony. He departed on December 28, 1700, with five other Englishmen, three male Indians and a "squaw." The party followed generally the Santee and Wateree Rivers.

In a little over three weeks, the expedition crossed into North Carolina in the Waxhaws. In the dead of winter, the explorers found ice on the streams near present-day Monroe. Some days later they visited the Catawba Indians. Following the old Trading Path, worn clear by the Indians, the party visited areas near the present cities of Charlotte, Kannapolis, Salisbury and Lexington. Turning eastward, in what is now Randolph County, Lawson and his fellow travelers visited Keyauwee Town, an Indian settlement rediscovered by University of North Carolina archaeologists in recent decades.

Further to the east, Lawson and a portion of the group (several had separated to go northward into Virginia) arrived at Occaneechee Town, now Hillsborough, from where a kindly Indian called Enoe Will guided them through the Tuscarora country to Richard Smith's plantation on Pamlico River near Washington. There on February 23 the exploratory trip ended. In approximately nine weeks the party had traversed only a little over half the thousand miles that Lawson estimated; still, in winter, on foot, the accomplishment was remarkable.

From explorer, John Lawson now became a settler. He built a house beside an Indian town near the present site of New Bern. Apparently well trained as a surveyor, he followed this trade, working as an assistant to Edward Mosely, the surveyor general of the province. But he also occupied his time touching up his journal, and in 1709 he sailed for England to arrange for its publication.

Titled *A New Voyage to Carolina*, his book provided a fascinating description of the Indian country. Since its first edition, it has gone through many republications. It has also been plagiarized by various writers, including John Brickell and William Byrd.

Lawson can be credited with helping found two North Carolina towns—Bath and New Bern. A landowner at Bath, he was one of its three commissioners when, in 1705, it became the first incorporated town in North Carolina. While in London for the publication of his book, Lawson became acquainted with Baron Von Graffenried, who was persuaded to select the junction of the Neuse and Trent Rivers—where Lawson then lived—as the location for a settlement of Palatines. Lawson sailed with about six hundred fifty Palatines early in 1710 and, upon arrival, he laid out the town that became known as New Bern.

The following year, the surveyor persuaded Von Graffenried and a black servant to accompany him on a trip into Tuscarora country for the purpose of finding a new route to Virginia. The journey, taken during the year in which the Tuscaroras had risen against the whites, was disastrous. The three men were captured and taken to the village of Catechna on Contentnea Creek, near the present Snow Hill. After an Indian-style trial that acquitted the travelers, an argument broke out. Both white men were then sentenced to death, though only Lawson was killed.

Tradition alternately reported that he was hanged, that his throat was cut and that thousands of splinters were stuck into his body and then set afire. Von Graffenried was fortunate enough to win his release and write his version of the event, which was, not surprisingly, uncomplimentary to Lawson's behavior. Von Graffenried proved that history tends to favor those who leave their own viewpoints in writing.

The Buggymobile
Built in New Bern

A VEHICLE BELIEVED TO HAVE BEEN the first automobile constructed in North Carolina was built by Gilbert S. Waters of New Bern in 1899.

Waters and his father were engaged in the prosperous business of manufacturing buggies in New Bern when in 1899 Gilbert visited Baltimore, where for the first time he saw "horseless carriages" driven by steam engines.

Excited by the idea of a self-propelled carriage, he returned to New Bern and within the year had completed his own machine, which, unlike the horseless carriages he had seen in Baltimore, was powered by a gasoline engine. The original "Buggymobile, " as Waters called his vehicle, was quite a success.

On the day of its first demonstration the streets were cleared and a skeptic is reported to have said, "He may get it started—but he will never stop it!" He did get it started and, in Waters' own words, "On my first test I raced down Main Street at twelve miles an hour." Though no specific account remains, he apparently had no trouble stopping it either.

Encouraged by his initial success, Waters was ready to convert his buggy factory into an automobile plant and "make buggymobiles by the thousands." His enthusiasm, however, was not shared by those who could have provided the financial backing. His father grew tired of his "senseless experiments" with horseless carriages and withdrew from the firm.

A local banker laughed at the idea of a self-propelled buggy, and Waters was told that horses and buggies would always be used and that buggies without horses would never be practical. They would be too expensive and dangerous, his critics claimed. Another banker is reported to have said, "You are doing well enough in the buggy business. You had better let well enough alone."

Unable to secure backing for such a radical venture, Waters reluctantly went back to making buggies. Meanwhile Henry Ford opened his automobile plant in Detroit and the first "Model T" Fords came on the market.

Although he was unable to put his creation into production for the public, Gilbert Waters' personal interest and faith in self-propelled road vehicles did not diminish. His first "Buggymobile" was soon worn out, and he built a new one in 1903. According to some accounts, it utilized the same engine that had been in the earlier model. It was this vehicle that Mr. Waters personally drove for over thirty-five years and that repeatedly gained national attention.

In 1939, when the car was thirty-six years old and Waters was seventy, he was invited to carry the vehicle to New York and appear as a guest on the nationwide radio program, *We The People*. Asked by host Gabriel Heatter if the car would still run, he replied, "It runs as good as it did thirty-six years ago. I can still hit thirty-five miles an hour in it, and I get forty miles to the gallon. That's better mileage than most streamlined cars get (and) I think mine is better looking too. "

To strengthen the credibility of his remarks, Waters then cranked the "Buggymobile" for the radio audience and the sound of its engine was heard from coast to coast on CBS.

Reflecting on the days just after the turn of the century, Waters said in 1939, "When I used to ask people to ride with me I would often get funny answers. They refused to 'risk their lives' with me. They held tightly on the seats when they did go and looked scared to death. A fat woman that weighed about two hundred pounds screamed bloody murder from the time she got in until she landed safely back at home. "

The "Buggymobile" which Gilbert S. Waters built in New Bern in 1903 and was still driving four decades later is now in the North Carolina Museum of History in Raleigh. Its builder died in February 1950.

Sir Walter Raleigh's Death

OCTOBER 29 IS THE ANNIVERSARY of the beheading in 1618 of Sir Walter Raleigh (spelled "Ralegh" in his day), sponsor of the first attempted English settlement of America at Roanoke Island.

A soldier, explorer, historian and author, Raleigh was once a powerful man in Queen Elizabeth's court, and certainly he was one of England's most revered statesmen. But he lived at a time when the crown rested tenuously on one head. It was also a time when England was in a continuing struggle for supremacy of the seas.

The beginning of Sir Walter's downfall came with the crowning of James I as king. Raleigh, never an admirer of James, was accused of complicity in a plot, presumably involving Spanish aid, to depose the king and bring to power Arabella Stuart.

In the trial, Raleigh pleaded in vain to be allowed to face his accuser. But English justice was bent to favor the king, and the courtier was convicted in 1603 and given this horrible sentence: "to be hanged and cut down alive, and your body shall be opened, your heart and bowels plucked out, and your privy members cut off and thrown into the fire before your eyes; then your head to be stricken off from your body and your body shall be divided into four quarters to be disposed of at the King's pleasure . . ." With such a sentence, it was hardly necessary for the chief justice to add, "and God have mercy on your soul."

A last hour reprieve (not pardon) saved Sir Walter this time, and he was sentenced to the Tower, England's jail for illustrious prisoners. With considerable freedom in the Tower, Raleigh remained one of the nation's idols, and among those who sought his counsel and friendship was Prince Henry, the young son of the king. When Henry died in 1612—possibly from poison administered by his father's supporters—Raleigh appeared to be doomed to spend the remainder of his life in prison.

In the Tower, Raleigh wrote his *History of the World* and several other works. The theme of his history, one author has said, is that "our desires and passions are generally too strong and too clever to be fully understood or controlled by reason."

Raleigh's influence even in jail haunted King James, so at the age of sixty-five, Sir Walter was allowed to leave the Tower on condition that he lead an expedition to Guiana in search for gold with which to replenish the royal treasury. He was strictly ordered to avoid any clash with the Spanish, whose favor James was seeking in an effort to arrange a wife for his young son Charles.

It was an ailing Raleigh that led the expedition with such great hope. Upon arrival on the coast of South America, Raleigh remained near the mouth of the river while part of his fleet, led by his young son Walter, continued up the Orinoco in search of gold.

The force was attacked by the Spanish, and the Englishmen had no choice but to respond. In the ensuing battle, young Walter (called Wat) was killed, a Spanish settlement was sacked and papers were captured from the Spanish which told the awful truth: that Raleigh had been "set up" by his own king who had furnished the Spanish with full details of the expedition. James I had made sure that either Raleigh would be killed by the Spanish, or that he would return to England a traitor for disobeying the royal directives.

Disconsolate over his son's death and cognizant that he had been betrayed, Raleigh's fleet sailed by way of Newfoundland to his homeland. He might have escaped by accepting the protection of the French, but that would have meant committing the very treason that he had been accused of fifteen years before.

The old sentence of 1603 was ordered carried out, and on October 29, 1618, Sir Walter Raleigh mounted the execution platform. He examined the axe and ordered the executioner to drop it when he stretched out his hands.

Raleigh's popularity among the people caused the king to refrain from invoking the original sentence of mutilation, and his wife Bess was allowed to claim his body. She buried the body but embalmed the head and kept it by her side for years. Ultimately the head was lost, and its whereabouts remain a mystery.

Raleigh is memorialized in North Carolina by the name of the capital city and in the great Sir Walter Raleigh Collection at University of North Carolina—Chapel Hill. The collection, housed in two rooms with seventeenth-century paneling and furniture of the period, is the most outstanding accumulation of Raleighana in the world and contains, among its hundreds of books, four copies of the exceedingly rare first edition of his *History of the World*. A large wooden statue of Raleigh, believed to be the work of Grinling Gibbons, is the most commanding of the various artifacts and art objects of the collection.

About the Author

In 2002 Dr. H.G. Jones was honored with the North Carolina Award, the highest honor the state of North Carolina can bestow upon a civilian. The following text taken from the award presentation chronicles his professional career and achievements:

H.G. Jones grew up in a house without books to become one of the most prolific writers and distinguished archivists in North Carolina. He has dedicated his life to forging a vision for the state's future by collecting and preserving every scrap of its past. For his relentless pursuit of North Carolina history, H.G. Jones receives the 2002 North Carolina Award for Public Service.

Jones was born in 1924 on a tenant farm in the Caswell County community of Kill Quick and endured the Great Depression under tough circumstances. Undeterred, he headed to Lees-McRae College; however, with the onset of World War II, he soon moved from the classroom to a U.S. Navy ship.

Following his discharge in 1946, Jones resumed his formal education, graduating magna cum laude from Appalachian State University, which honored him twenty-two years later with its first Distinguished Alumnus Award. He went on to earn advanced degrees from George Peabody College (M.A.) and Duke University (Ph.D.).

In 1956, Jones accepted a position in Raleigh as state archivist with the N.C. Department of Archives and History where he developed the largest and most comprehensive state archival and records management program in the country. This accomplishment was recognized in 1964 when the Society of American

Archivists presented its first Distinguished Service Award to the department. Jones was named president of the society in 1968, and became the only person to twice receive the Waldo G. Leland Prize, the organization's top award for a book on archival history, theory and practice. That same year, he became director of the Department of Archives and History, a position he held until 1974. During his directorship, the department grew, vastly expanding its services, obtaining funds for a new records center and developing additional state historic sites.

For the next twenty years, Jones served as curator of the North Carolina Collection and adjunct professor of history at the University of North Carolina at Chapel Hill. He retired from those positions in 1993 to become part-time Thomas W. Davis Research Historian, a title he still holds. He also continues to keep an eye on the state's historical programs as an emeritus member of the N.C. Historical Commission.

The jewel of his career is the North Carolina Collection, a staggering array of published materials pertaining to North Carolina and its inhabitants. The collection is by far the most comprehensive of its kind in the country. While managing the collection and the North Caroliniana Society, a nonprofit organization he founded in 1975, Jones continued his prolific writing, including his award-winning book *North Carolina Illustrated, 1524-1984*.

In 1971, while on his first vacation, Jones discovered the second great passion in his life—the Arctic and its native people. For the past thirty-one years, he has traveled to the area to study, collect, and write about the culture and art of the Eskimoans, amassing over time an unmatched collection of Inuit art and artifacts.

Today, Dr. Jones continues to live near the UNC campus with his lifetime collection of North Carolina and Arctic literature, art and memorabilia.

About the Co-editors

THE CO-EDITORS ARE FATHER and daughter. They are not related to Dr. H.G. Jones.

K. Randell Jones is a writer and leadership consultant living in Winston-Salem. Since earning a graduate business degree at UNC-Chapel Hill in 1985, he has adopted North Carolina as home.

His publications are:

In the Footsteps of Daniel Boone. John F. Blair, Publisher, spring 2005
Dangerous Opportunity: Making Change Work. (with Dr. Chris Musselwhite) Discovery Learning Press, 2004
Educational Program for the Overmountain Victory National Historic Trail. National Park Service, 2003
Footsteps for Freedom, the True Story of the Overmountain Men of 1780. OVTA, 2001
Welcome to the Albemarle-Pamlico. By the Way Travel Tapes, 1997
Welcome Home to North Carolina. By the Way Travel Tapes, 1995
Welcome to South Carolina's Historic Lowcountry. By the Way Travel Tapes, 1995
Welcome the Gaston County—The Magnolia Tour. By the Way Travel Tapes, 1994
Welcome to South Carolina's Old 96 District, 1994,

Caitlin D. Jones is a junior at Salem Academy, Winston-Salem, North Carolina and a Native Tar Heel.

A SOUTHERN SCHOOL-HOUSE.

Original Publication Dates